Where Were You When I Was Hurting?

Where Were You When I Was Hurting?

BY NICKY CRUZ

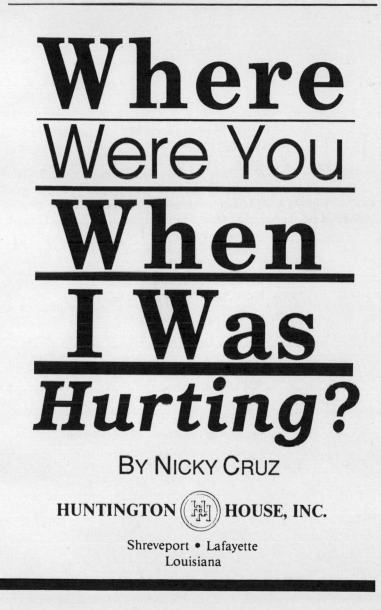

HUNTINGTON HOUSE, INC.

Shreveport • Lafayette
Louisiana

Huntington House, Inc.
1200 N. Market St., Shreveport, LA 71107

Library of Congress Catalog Card Number 86-81416

ISBN Number 0-910311-41-2

Cover by Don Ellis
Typography by Publications Technologies

Printed in the United States of America

Table of Contents

Dedication

To Sonny Arguinzoni and his precious wife, Julie. Sonny was one of the first fruits of my ministry. He is my spiritual son. God has made Sonny an oasis in a wounded and rejected society — and for this, I rejoice. Sonny's church, Victory Outreach, has become one of the greatest refuges today for the hurting and needy. People come to hear the Word of God and to be fed, clothed and healed. What a Holy Ghost Hospital! His ministry is expanding throughout major cities in the United States and Europe. He has become one of my inspirations and motivations to continue preaching, knowing there may be another "Sonny" out in the crowd. Sonny, this book is dedicated to you because I love you, respect you and think of you as my own brother. You are my best friend.

Acknowledgments

A special acknowledgment to Rob Kerby of Publications Technologies. You have done a truly fabulous and magnificent job in rewriting and revising these stories.

Thanks also to Mrs. Madeline Harris for your many hours of diligent editing work.

To my wife, Gloria — Thank you for your inspiration and encouragement as I worked on this book. Also for helping in the parts where I needed the feminine touch and knowledge of a woman.

To June Creswell — Thank you for your ideas, research, long hours of work and sacrifice.

To Cindy Irwin — Thank you for typing, retyping, rewriting and listening to hundreds of hours of tapes.

I pray these friends will be recompensed by God for the hard work they have all done on this book.

I

It's Lonely Out There

1

Mary

When I was 15 or so, the graying widow with the pain in her voice had an annoying habit of dispensing advice at me in the hallway of our Brooklyn tenement.

As a street-wise kid, I didn't listen.

I didn't want to be seen with her. I tried to restrict our contact to increasingly unavoidable greetings outside my room.

But the woman was strangely, perhaps involuntarily drawn to me.

Why?

I had no idea.

I didn't like her.

Her advice — offered in a thick German accent — was unsolicited and unwelcome. I was a junior high school dropout, living on adolescent adrenaline and young, macho passions.

I was proud, yet afraid.

I was feared on the streets — yet just an unsure boy, scared of the big city, a newcomer in the ranks of the Mau Maus — one of the most vicious street gangs in Brooklyn's Fort Greene slums.

Incredibly, old Mary seemed to yearn for my friendship — even just my acknowledgment that she existed. But that was just too much to expect of a swaggering kid. I had no friendship to give her. She was just a crazy old lady — something pretty common on the streets in New York.

Today, I know that behind her dowdy exterior and her bold-yet-fearful hallway greetings, Mary was calling out not only to me —

But to a memory ...

To someone lost to her forever.

She was begging me for a moment of kindness, a word. But we were from different worlds. I was finding my teen-age identity as a would-be hoodlum wielding a fancy cane and strutting in an embroidered gang "letter jacket."

My friends were hyped and going nowhere in a frenzy — sprinting across dirty alleys and rooftops, dodging cops, ambushing rival gangs, jitterbugging with death ... desperate not to miss any of our life's frantic thrills, wildly trying out all our young whims and lusts.

I didn't want anybody to see me talking to an old woman.

Yet, Mary persisted.

She didn't go after anybody else.

Just me.

She wanted to try to mother me, I feared.

I wasn't interested.

I'd had enough of that from my spirit-summoning, witchcraft-professing, "healer" mother.

Mary was nuts, I thought.

Nuts.

Why else would a tattered old recluse seek friendship with a dead-end kid in love with violence, filled with bitterness — bewildered over being packed off to New York by parents who didn't know what to do about his petty crime and growing rebellion back in rural Puerto Rico?

I had nothing to give Mary. I was supposed to be staying with my brother, Frank. But, I chose to live on my own, spending my days and nights in the exciting, violent, crime-filled streets.

Although I would have scoffed at the idea then, I see now that Mary and I had much in common.

I spoke halting English with a thick accent that betrayed my roots and my virtual illiteracy. Her voice branded her as an outsider, too.

I was deeply homesick and lonely at night. In the darkness of my dirty room, I longed for my beautiful island in the Caribbean and my sister and 17 brothers.

And Mary, in the lonely night, talked aloud — seemingly to herself — crying her loneliness to the thin walls.

I tried to shut out the haunting sounds of her grief. I wrote her off as crazy.

It wasn't within my self-image to show concern about her pain, her loneliness, her ache to entertain a house full of rowdy, laughing relatives, to gently chide her handsome, German husband for neglecting to wipe the mud off his boots as they leaned back in front of a warm, crackling fireplace ...

No, Mary didn't belong in New York, alone, abandoned in our neighborhood's daily exploitation of the unwary, its unrelenting din of music and anger, its mocking, uncaring self-destruction and its casual, everyday violence.

She belonged in a cozy country house in Bavaria or maybe a big brownstone — or its 300-year-old equivalent — in Dresden or Danzig or Frankfurt.

Back then, I didn't know anything about that — not that I would have cared.

Well ...

I might have been curious. But I would have felt no pity. I wouldn't have cared that her world was one of tradition, of black shawls and antique lace.

Of Sabbath candles.

Of hearty laughter and celebration.

Of heritage.

In our New York tenement, her longing and her fears were real and desperate.

Unending.

Unsalved.

Unrelieved.

In the dubious safety of her room, she waited alone through Brooklyn's cold night ... alone, exiled behind her dismal walls in one of the worst of the borough's decaying, firetrap districts.

Mary was a misfit — pathetic, but defiant, drawing no pity from a sneering city.

Yet, silent to others, she would greet me.

I would respond and brush past.

I didn't want to talk.

I didn't want to hear her commentary on my life. She was crazy. She was old. I wanted nothing of her.

So, behind her locked and bolted door, she mourned alone. As a 15-year-old, I had no idea of just how real and desperate were her fears and pains in the early morning stillness. I only heard her moaning, her weeping, her crying out just one thin wall away from my bed.

And I closed my eyes to the reality that she and I had a great deal in common.

To be needed.

To forgive.

To experience God's healing that comes with giving up old hatred and pain and unforgiveness. Neither of us knew anything about that, however.

Not yet.

We were still strangers in a Mecca of child hookers, a Sodom and Gomorrah of unending pain, an American black hole of Calcutta.

She needed to forgive. To feel the joy of release.

Instead, she clutched onto her hurt — wailing in the night for a life long gone.

And she was ignored.

In a city of 10 million people, there was no one who cared about Mary.

Least of all me.

At night, I hated her.

I screamed at her through my apartment walls — threatening her if the wailing, the moaning, the crying didn't stop. I pounded on her door, ready to crash into her room and strangle the haunting, eerie weeping invading my insomnia.

She only wanted the caress of her husband — or to once again cry with her two little boys.

I only wanted to sleep.

I didn't care about her murdered family.

In the dim light of her tiny room, she would finger their browned, flaking snapshots. And she would ache.

They were dead.

Gassed at Auschwitz or Dachau or one of those other dark depots of Hitler's Final Solution.

Alone, Mary wept.

In the cold Brooklyn night — her pitiful muttering intruded into my darkness.

My curses and wall-pounding usually brought stunned stillness.

Then, just as I was dozing off, the mourning would start up again. And I would scream threats.

And it would stop again.

I can tell you exactly where I was when Mary was hurting.

I hated the lonely widow.

At 3 a.m., I would lurch into my room — drunk and bloody — angry, excited, wasted emotionally and physically, craving the peace of sleep.

As I punched my pillow, her moaning would rise — ghostly, grating on my drug-frayed nerves.

For three years, I hated her for her pain and, frankly, I didn't want to know what was troubling her.

As I rushed back and forth from my room, she watched my downward spiral into recreational drugs, everyday crime and exploitive sex.

She would call out her advice.

But I didn't hear.

Daily she ventured fearfully onto Brooklyn's hostile sidewalk, defying her own great emptiness, daring to trust none of the ignoring faces — shuffling aloofly to the next-door grocery ... ignoring the catcalls of the kids and the irritated glares of hurrying strangers.

She trusted no one — there was potential danger behind every smile. She knew well that anyone coming too close probably was eyeing her limp, frayed purse or sizing up whether it would be worth it to snatch her small packages.

One afternoon, I needed money badly.

I knew her apartment would be easy to burglarize while she was out. I figured she had money behind that locked door.

A fellow gang member and I watched closely for her to leave. In what seemed like an eternity, she fumbled with the bolt, then shuffled downstairs and out.

We ran to her door and broke it open. Frantically we searched for hiding places where she might have stashed her savings.

"Look in the stove and refrigerator — even the matchbox," I ordered. "Anywhere she might hide cash." Then, as I fumbled through a dresser drawer, I began to laugh. "Manny!" I called, "Come here."

The drawer was full of faded old pictures. Her husband. Her parents. Two little boys. All in Germany in the 1930s and 1940s.

In one photo she was holding both of the kids.

We hooted scornfully at the stupid relics of her past.

Then I found what I was looking for. Carefully wrapped in a handkerchief was $280. Stuffing it into my pocket, I went to the refrigerator, drank some milk and strolled out the broken door.

When Mary returned, she knew immediately what had happened. She called the police and pointed to the mute evidence. Naturally, they questioned me, but I told them in innocent fashion, "I don't know nuthin'. I wasn't even around when it happened."

With no grounds to keep me, they let me go.

And that was that.

Yet ...

The guilt of that particular burglary stayed with me over the years. And after I came to know Jesus years later, my conscience became increasingly sensitive to it. I had to make things right with old advice-dispensing Mary.

Why?

Why? Not because robbing her was the worst thing I had ever done. God knows it probably was one of my least offenses. There just remained something deep in my heart that wouldn't let me forget what I had done to a helpless, hurting old woman.

During my second year of Bible college, I returned to New York City for three months to witness in the streets before returning for my third year.

High on my priority list was to make restitution with Mary.

So, I made my way back to the old neighborhood. Things were just as bad — maybe worse. Why she would choose to stay in the decaying, graffiti-defiled tenement was hard to figure.

Inside as I approached her apartment, I could still see old evidence of the damage I had done to that ancient door.

I knocked.

There was no answer.

I knocked again.

And again.

Then I heard that familiar, fear-filled German voice. "Who's there?" she called hesitantly from behind the bolted door.

"It's Nicky. Remember old Nicky?"

There was silence.

I didn't know if she would just choose to ignore me. There was no answer.

Then, there were muffled sounds of arthritic hands fumbling with the bolts and locks.

Her astonished face peered out at me.

"Why, Nicky!" Mary blurted, much more friendly than I had anticipated.

After all, there was no reason that she should even remember me. "I didn't ever expect to see you again," she said as she looked me over.

"Hello," I said, uneasy in the littered hallway. "You know —" I fumbled awkwardly. "Mary, I've been saving my money so I could pay back the $280 I robbed you of years ago. You probably didn't even know I did it."

"Yes, I knew you did it, Nicky."

She did? Then why was she so friendly to me back then?

And so open now?

I hung my head.

"I was afraid you might," I murmured. "Here's your money, Mary."

Although I tried to hand it to her, she didn't make a move to take it. Instead, she opened the door wide and said,

"Come into my apartment, Nicky."

In our slum, this is not an invitation that one makes to everyone — particularly to known ex-delinquents.

I stepped inside.

It was hard to know what to say as she continued to look me over, obviously very pleased by my presence. Finally words came to me in the awkward stillness.

"Can I ask you one thing, Mary?" I asked. "Why did you always talk to yourself so much? Why did you cry every night?"

It was a very personal question asked rather bluntly — but she didn't seem to be offended.

She led me over to her collection of pictures and pointed to two little boys nestled in her protective arms. Although the picture was faded with the years, life and joy could still be seen in their eyes.

"There are my children, Nicky. They died a long time ago."

Murdered, she said, softly.

Murdered as — naked, coughing and crying — they clutched onto their daddy. Around them, a Nazi concentration camp's "showers" filled with poisonous gas.

She picked up a picture of a handsome, dark, young man.

Looking longingly at it for a moment, she finally handed it to me.

"This is my husband," she said. "He died, too."

"I'm so sorry," was all I could manage.

"Because we were Jews, Nicky, all of my family was destroyed."

I was stunned.

For years I had lived next to a broken victim of one of history's most terrible brutalities — World War II's Jewish Holocaust. And I hadn't known or cared.

I had thought only of my sleep.

I had even robbed her.

Her voice broke. "How I hate the world for taking away my husband and my precious children."

I nodded, the horror of it all sinking in.

"I was raped, abused and tortured," she was saying. "My children were tortured, too, and my husband ..."

She paused. I wept inside. Now I understood the anguish that had tormented Mary night after night.

While I pounded on the wall.

"One of the soldiers used me," she was saying, "... treated me like a dog. I broke away from him and ran. Soon after that, Germany was defeated and we were freed."

My guilt overpowered me.

I had shunned her.

I had abused her.

I had hated her — this fragile remnant of God's chosen people.

"In the night I long for my children and my husband," she told me, handing me more old photographs. "Early every morning, I kneel at my altar praying and weeping for them."

I knew.

Oh, did I know.

I had heard her too many mornings not to understand. "Mary," I struggled out. "You've lived with all this pain for so long."

I bit my lip. "I thought you ... you were a mental case as I watched you. Whenever I saw you walk out of this apartment, you didn't seem to care about anybody. It was almost as if you didn't know anyone was around, or that you wanted people to avoid you."

She nodded, trembling — but touched by my concern, obviously gratified that finally, FINALLY, I cared.

"Mary, why didn't you leave this place? Why didn't you have the police arrest me when I robbed you? You could have complained to the landlord and he'd have kicked me out for being such a threat to everyone."

She shook her head, the shadow of a smile creasing her face.

"Nicky, you were my only security. Everyone was scared of you. I knew I would be protected. This was your 'turf.' If anybody tried to hurt me, I knew down deep you would take care of them."

The irony swept over me. She hadn't reported me because she was trusting me to protect her.

"Why didn't you hate me, Mary?"

There was a sudden twinkle in her eyes. "Because you look so much like one my children, Nicky. Every time I saw you, I wanted to hug you."

"How could you see your son in me?" I exclaimed. "I'm so dark and you're so fair."

"My husband was a very dark-complected Jew."

A lot of things made sense.

I saw how a lonely old woman had been drawn to a vicious street kid.

I understood.

"Mary," I said, "I'm a Christian now. I have given my heart to Jesus Christ and that's the reason I'm returning your money. For the first time, I can look at you with love and compassion. Please take the money I've saved for so long."

She shook her head. "No, Nicky, I don't want it."

I took her hands and placed the money in them.

She hesitated a moment.

Then, "I can't help but notice a difference in you, Nicky," she said. "You're so happy and smiling. I had seen on TV and in the newspaper articles that something had happened to you."

Suddenly, she became defensive.

"I don't believe what you believe, Nicky. Let's keep it that way."

"But Mary, I'm living proof of a new birth through Jesus Christ, the promised Messiah."

"No, no!" she cried. "I don't believe that."

Seeing her consternation and not wanting to antagonize her, I just said, "Mary, I don't want to argue with you. I just want to tell you that I love you and want you to forgive me for what I did to you."

Tears began flowing down her wrinkled cheeks. "Nicky, before you leave, please let me kiss you good-bye."

Before you leave ...? The meaning of the words sank in: She didn't *want* to know Jesus.

She didn't want to give up her pain or her unforgiveness of those who had snatched love and joy from her life.

For a moment, I felt awkward. I was 21 years old and Mary was over 70. I had never known love from my mother. She had never known the love of an adult son.

I reached out to her and drew her face close to mine. Her tears mingled with my tears as she gently kissed my cheek.

"Mary," I said, "As a favor to both you and me, may I say a little prayer for you before I leave?"

She agreed.

I took her hands in mine and closed my eyes. "Oh, God, bear Mary's pain," I whispered. "Let her know that you are the God of Abraham, Isaac and Jacob. Move and minister to her in those deep areas that human hands cannot touch. Will you please, Jesus, put your lips on her hurting wounds and kiss her pain away? Let Mary know that you have always been there to help her and that you love her so much. Heal her, Lord, from this bitterness and loneliness. Help her see you as a Jesus that has compassion for others."

As I left her apartment and walked the streets of my old haunts again, I felt lighter and freer than I ever had before.

I had returned the money.

Mary had forgiven me.

And now I forgave myself.

I mourned, too. She had firmly rejected any discussion of the Lord who had transformed me.

Instead of accepting the Promised Land of God's wonderful Messiah, she chose to remain in the Egypt of her bitterness.

I'd had a heart-rending glimpse inside the ravages of her great loneliness ... a decades-old anguish that literally had eaten Mary's joy of life away.

Nobody could really know the agony behind her heart's closed doors.

Nobody ever would.

Mary died as she lived most of her life — in fear behind her locked door, miserably lonely, suspicious and aloof.

After I graduated from Bible school, I returned to New York with Gloria, my bride, and took her to meet Mary.

But Mary had died two months after I'd come back with her money.

As Gloria and I walked away from the apartment, I recounted Mary's lifelong misery — and her choice to mourn for 40 years rather than go on with life.

"Why do so many people suffer from loneliness?" I asked myself. Being newly married, I couldn't fathom it.

But today, 25 years later — having weathered severe loneliness myself, I now understand.

Yes, I understand.

And I know this, too: We don't have to be lonely. God doesn't decide for us that we must spend years alone.

Loneliness is not from God.

We have a choice.

Loneliness ...

Or forgiveness and life.

2

It's Lonely Out There

Some people cannot understand Mary's void. But many of us do — and have experienced similar loneliness and bitterness.

Yes, we say, her grief was justified.

She had been wronged.

She deserved to hate her tormentors.

She had a right to mourn the life that was stripped away from her.

Or did she?

The Lord tells us there is a time to laugh ... and a time to weep. A time to die — and a time to mourn.

But for 40 years?

Do we have a right to destroy ourselves with sorrow and self-pity?

No — no more than we are permitted to lift a gun to our head and bring life to an end.

Mary had a choice between life and death. After a normal time of working through her very legitimate anguish, her broken heart could have been mended. She could have picked up the pieces and moved forward — despite the horror, the terror, the pain that she had suffered.

But Mary refused to forgive or go on.

She chose death.

For the rest of her life, she remained the same as on the day she lost her family — nurturing her anger and self-pity and bitterness; reveling in her sorrow, her self-centeredness and her loneliness.

She made a choice.

She chose to remain at the death camp for the rest of her life.

She chose.

So can you. Daily we each choose to forgive and go on.

Or to refuse — deceiving ourselves that it's better to remain in our pain; believing that there is sweet peace in revenge.

You know, I am constantly amazed at the clever deceits our human minds devise. Sometimes these lies to ourselves seem harmless. But they destroy us, as they did Mary. She hung onto the deceit that she had every right to remember and relive her horror and to hate her tormentors.

Nightly she mourned — weeping and crying out to God, but not seeking his answers — instead remaining enveloped in her self-pity.

Have you ever done the same thing?

Have you ever trapped yourself in self-destructive behavior, simply because you are accustomed to wallowing in your problems rather than solving them?

Don't feel so all alone.

We all pretend that we're ignoring our deep hurts.

But we don't really ignore them.

They gnaw at us.

And we end up wallowing in them more than before.

But we don't have to.

There is healing in forgiveness.

My robbing Mary bothered me for years. It would remain unresolved — as guilt and self-pity — until the Lord Jesus reached down into my rotten life and until I experienced not only his forgiveness, but hers.

Basic to all causes for loneliness is this miserable root of self-pity. "Poor me — I did a terrible thing, I robbed a widow of her life savings. Poor me. Poor me. I'm worthless. Poor me."

Mary felt sorry for herself, too — and who wouldn't under the circumstances?

But can we waste a lifetime feeling sorry for ourselves? Of course not. Life must go on.

Mary basically died right there in the death camp. Her life ended. Her remaining 40 years were wasted, unused. Her potential was undeveloped. She retreated into her anguish.

Instead of celebrating her escape — she lived in the death of her family, reveling in the self-pity, the anguish, the self-centered grief. "Poor me, poor me, poor me. They murdered my husband and my little boys." It consumed her.

What can you or I do to avoid the predicament Mary placed herself into for 40 years?

Get tough with yourself.

Forgive.

Forgive.

Then go on with life.

We are commanded to love those who do terrible things to us.

That may seem impossible.

But there is great healing, release and joy in such forgiveness.

Those people and the hurt they caused us suddenly no longer control us. We no longer wallow in self-pity. We no longer relive the pain of what they did.

We forgive.

Forgive yourself, too, if you were less than an angel in the whole thing.

Most importantly, take the whole thing to the Lord. Ask him to help you forgive.

Pray for the person who hurt you.

Ask the Lord to bless them.

Whew!

That's not easy, is it?

But you'll be surprised at what happens to your attitude toward them when you start praying for them.

Careful, however: never pray that they will get their due — or that God will let them fry in hell for the dirt they did to you.

We're not permitted to condemn anyone.

That's God's role.

We're to love those who spitefully use us. To walk a second mile. To turn the other cheek.

To love one another.

The alternative is to live like Mary did.

A bitter, unforgiving spirit is a terrible thing. Mary allowed pity and bitterness to destroy her life. They kept her locked in that tenement, her self-centered life meaning nothing to anybody.

Such self-pity has one simple, demonic source. Yes, Satan plots together with his evil forces to our internal — as well as eternal — destruction.

Of course, when we are wronged, we do not feel like forgiving. So, the key to forgiveness lies in forgetting how we feel and recognizing what we are commanded to do.

To forgive.

3

How Can I Fight Back?

Forgiveness begins with our will. We must set our wills to forgive, regardless of the "right and wrong" aspect of actions against us.

If we get hung up there — trying to be the judge of those who hurt us — we'll never achieve forgiveness.

Remember, God is the judge.

We don't have to take our grievances against others before him. The Bible says that Satan does that constantly — particularly accusing believers.

Instead, we have to leave the wrongdoing with the Lord.

It has to stay with him.

We're not God.

He alone is.

And he knows what needs to be done.

And remember, he wants to forgive that person, just like he forgave you in all your sins — if they will seek it.

So, let go of your accusation.

Give it up.

It's God's business, not yours.

What do you lose when you forgive someone who has done something awful to you?

Your pride, mostly.

You don't get your revenge.

Well, guess what God has said about that?

Vengeance is his.

Not ours.

So, step away from this pride — this loss of face, this nagging temptation to even the score.

If we maintain a constantly forgiving spirit, we also break free from the terrible prison of loneliness.

That's right.

So, let me repeat: there is incredible healing in forgiveness.

Forgiveness is the answer to loneliness.

Unforgiveness traps us — filling us with things such as a critical, negative outlook, that nasty view of life that tightens our iron grip of loneliness.

Step away from criticism.

Find good, not bad.

Live in the positives — not the negatives.

When we are critical of someone, our spirit shuts them out. They sense our rejection even though it may be unspoken. They in turn shut us out. As we allow this critical attitude to permeate our lives, we find ourselves deep in the pits of loneliness.

We keep wondering why no one wants to be around us.

Well, the answer should be obvious.

Who wants to be around a complainer, a constant critic, a moaner ... a wailer in the night?

In our unforgiveness, we let self-pity bloom and criticism bubble forth.

And people aren't comfortable in our company. Can you blame them?

Who wants to spend time with a self-centered, self-pitying, negative, criticizing crybaby?

When our lives totally revolve around "me and mine" and all the injustice done to us and ours — there simply isn't room for anyone else.

People who are interested only in their affairs cannot reach out to others and form satisfying relationships.

As you forgive and start your life anew, becoming interested in other people may be an effort at first.

But God made us social beings.

We need each other.

The Bible warns believers not to forsake fellowship — instead to gather together to share each other's joys and sorrow.

But remember that — more importantly than anything — we will fail miserably if we try to do any of this in our own strength.

Only God can change us.

If we struggle in our own energies, we can only fail.

Ask him to help you forgive.

Ask him to help you break your habits of negative conversation — of self-centered, self-pitying, critical whimpering.

I've been lonely many times in my life.

I've known the pain.

Forgive.

Overcome self-pity.

With God's help, you will be an overcomer.

And when you do, life takes on a whole new dimension.

Experience God's marvelous healing.

Step away from the curse of loneliness.

Get on with your life.

Or ...

Or be like Mary.

Mary, Mary.

Where was I when you were hurting? I was a stupid 16-year-old all wrapped up in my own problems and my own hatreds and my own self-pity.

I couldn't see you, Mary.

I could only see me.

It's The Kids Who Suffer

4

Chico and Trini

Wheelchair-bound Chico was 10 or 11, the son of a prominent woman psychiatrist and atheist. Trini was a 12-year-old shoeshine boy and petty criminal.

I met the two boys when I was preaching to a crowd of 14,000 in a Mexico City coliseum right after the terrible earthquake of 1985.

It's a shame when an adult chooses to live in misery rather than forgiveness. But it's a horrible thing when an adult's unforgiving heart injures an innocent child. Trini and Chico were such victims.

In the ruins of Mexico City, God sovereignly intervened for both of them.

Trini's and Chico's miracles took place less than a week after the earthquake. We had already booked our crusade before the quake — which, if you remember, killed thousands and ravaged downtown Mexico City, even toppling skyscrapers. At first I didn't think we should go, but the Mexican Christians organizing the revival there begged us to come ahead. Now, more than ever, they said, Mexico needed Jesus.

As you can imagine there were enormous logistical problems in holding a big crusade in the middle of a national disaster. But the Lord worked it all out. Three days before the crusade, it looked impossible. Then, the Lord opened the way for us to use the coliseum. Still, many people thought nobody was going to come to a crusade — not with the city lying in ruins and people still buried under rubble.

But each night, we packed beyond capacity this coliseum designed to handle 14,000. If we had stayed there another five days, we would have had to move to the national soccer stadium, which could accommodate many times that. That's one of the frustrations of a schedule — something I'm already taking measures to change. I get upset when I have to go on and leave when revival is just bursting into flame. That's not going to happen again to me. I've determined that Jesus' work is much more important than me sticking to my appointments and my speaking schedule.

I should have stayed that time.

I will from now on.

Well, that night as I preached, I spotted lame Chico sitting on the front row in his wheelchair. A crippled little boy is a pitiful sight.

He should be running.

He should be playing. He should be laughing. Not sitting immobile.

But there was something even more striking about little Chico. The kid wasn't looking for healing.

He was earnestly looking for Jesus.

I wasn't preaching healing that night. I was preaching salvation — that's my calling. I don't believe that I have any special power to heal. I believe such things can happen through the prayer of all believers.

I had told this to the Mexican Christians working to organize the crusade. We had talked about how they have authority in Jesus' name to pray for each other — and for the sick.

That night as I invited people to come forward and confess Jesus as their Lord, we rather unexpectedly began to have miraculous healings.

A mother brought her little deaf-and-dumb child to the front for prayer.

As Mexican Christians at the altar laid hands on him, he spoke the first word in his life: "Jesus."

Then, he said "Mama," too.

His mother actually dropped him — she couldn't believe it. She cried out in joy, hugging him and us and praising God as the little boy kept grinning and talking.

Well, the effect was dramatic. The crowd could see exactly what God had done.

Then, there was a lady whose spine was healed — she had been disabled for 10 years. And a man who had a basketball-size growth in his stomach was healed. In front of thousands' eyes, the growth just disappeared as he was praying for salvation.

Most of the people who were healed had come forward to become Christians.

But Chico couldn't come forward at first.

Sitting there on the front row, he could see what was going on. As I remember, his atheist mother had brought him to the crusade just to humor him.

I don't know what the Holy Spirit had used to get Chico to insist that he had to go to the service. It was perhaps the *The Cross and the Switchblade* movie shown in a local theater or church. Actor Eric Estrada — who plays me in the movie — is very popular in Latin America. He's Hispanic and very macho and very well-known from the Spanish-dubbed reruns of the old *CHiPs* motorcycle-police TV show. So, sometimes people come to my crusades expecting to hear him preach.

They hear me instead.

Maybe that's what brought Chico into the stadium in a crowd of 14,000. I don't know for sure. Maybe his mother thought that a close-up view of religion would quell the boy's curiosity on the subject.

Well, instead of getting a good taste of the absurdity of Christianity, Chico got a deep drink of everlasting water.

And sitting there next to his scoffing mother, Chico decided to give everything to the Lord. The boy turned to her and announced that he wanted her to push his wheelchair down to the altar.

Surprised, she refused.

Well, Chico had seen the truth.

And he was certain it would set him free. The faith of a child is a magnificent thing. The Lord wasn't going to let Chico's mother's lack of belief hurt Chico this time.

Chico grew determined to respond to the altar call — when I invited those in the crowd to step forward and surrender their lives to Jesus.

But, Chico could not walk. One of his legs was eight inches shorter than it should have been.

He wasn't strong enough to push himself in his wheelchair. He was partially paralyzed.

But in the power of his newfound conviction, all that didn't matter to him.

He lurched out of his wheelchair.

And as the people on the front row stared, he began to cry out and shout —

As his leg grew.

I noticed what was happening as the boy careened toward the front.

He wasn't crawling.

He was walking — awkwardly but with growing assurance.

His leg had been fully restored, but he was walking — haltingly. That wasn't hard to explain: he was walking for the very first time in his whole life.

And he was excited.

He stepped toward us — looking as if he would fall at first. Then, he began to gain balance.

When he reached the altar, he told counselors there that as he had started to get up, he began to feel pain all over his body. He didn't know what it was.

Then he felt numb as he began to walk, he said.

As you can imagine, Chico came crying, proclaiming that Jesus Christ is Lord.

I don't have to tell you how Chico's situation was wonderfully miraculous. The Lord didn't allow the boy's mother's unforgiveness and stubbornness to keep the boy from accepting God's forgiveness.

The Lord let Chico bypass his mother's unbelief.

How I wish it could always be the case.

"The sins of the fathers shall be visited upon the children to the third and fourth generation" is a scripture I have not understood until lately.

How unjust, my heart used to cry out.

I looked at kids like Trini.

Trini was a Mexican pastor's son. The boy was working on the street after years of serious physical abuse by his father.

"I came because you and I are so much alike," Trini told me at our crusade in the coliseum. "I hate my father's guts."

I could only smile. How many times had I said the same thing as a 12-year-old? And it had been true. I had loved and respected my father — yet hated and feared him at the same time. My father had been a famous spiritualist healer, a witch-man. People had come to our house in rural Puerto Rico at all hours, seeking the healer who listened to good "white" demons and who would miraculously reach into their bodies and pull out masses of tumors.

My father had been deceived. There are no good demons.

Trini's abusive father claimed to be a pastor of the Gospel. Yet he inflicted severe wounds on the body of his adolescent son — and pushed the boy beyond human endurance so that Trini had run off to live on the street with the wrong sort of people.

Trini told us candidly that he was into drugs and alcohol — and that he smoked cigarettes habitually.

He was just a child.

A little boy.

Just as I had been.

A street urchin.

Trini gave his heart to the Lord at the crusade — and had his wrist healed, a wrist and elbow that couldn't straighten out after a beating by his father.

As I prayed with Trini, I was suddenly aware of the Lord's anointing on the boy. He was just a child, but the Lord already had blessed him with a rare eloquence and boldness. Joyfully, Trini proclaimed his new faith.

How could any man of God have abused this boy?

The scripture, "the sins of the fathers shall be visited upon the children to the third and fourth generation," again crossed my mind.

How unfair, I cried out to the Lord. Why should Trini have to go through what I'd gone through — just because of his father's sins?

How can we break this curse?

How can God punish innocent little children just because their parents choose to sin?

I saw the alcoholic mother and the criminal father. I saw atheistic parents, such as Chico's mother, refusing to let their children walk in God's light.

That just didn't seem right.

It wasn't fair.

What were the answers?

5

It's The Kids Who Suffer

The sins of the fathers shall be visited upon the children to the third and fourth generation.

What a frightening scripture.

I have four beautiful girls. It is my heart's desire that they be free to choose God-honoring lives — and not have to labor under any curse of my past sins and those of my father or my grandfather.

With Trini standing before me, telling us that he wished he could kill his brutal, evangelistic father, I felt my old doubts returning. That night, the Lord changed Trini forever, soothing the wrath in the boy's young heart for his vicious father — and healing the boy's arm.

But I began to seek the Lord for answers to this curse: "The sins of the fathers shall be visited upon the children to the third and fourth generation."

Since my ministry deals with troubled youth, I was in a prime situation to find the simple answer.

I saw it in the letters troubled kids and parents write me and in my numerous counseling sessions.

What was the Lord saying?

He showed me one sin in our particular society that hurts far more than all others. I cannot think of "sins of the fathers" without this hideous thing coming to mind.

Its name is incest.

If there is anything more damaging to children than this, I can't imagine it.

Perhaps I am more conscious of the life-long emotional trauma this sin produces because I encounter so much of it.

Working with youth today is like a clean-up operation after war. The dead and dying are strewn all over the battlefield. For many of these kids, no hope for restoration exists — not without God.

Left alone, they are terminally wounded, their spirits forever crushed and twisted.

All we can do is seek the Lord's wisdom to find the right thing to say or do. With so little time in which we can minister, so few Christians willing to help and with so many kids abused, I find myself stumbling through the spiritual Emergency Room, asking the Lord to show me those able to respond quickly to treatment.

I would venture to say that more than 95 percent of the problems of today's youth relate directly to the moral degeneracy of our society.

While movies, television, popular music, pornography, drugs and the like contribute to the terrible corruption of this generation — one thing stands out as a great destroyer of young souls.

Incest.

Children are at the mercy of the evil, self-seeking adults from whom they cannot escape.

A large percentage of their tormentors are within their own homes.

Consider Kathy, a young woman who came to us suffering from anorexia nervosa — an increasingly common disorder in which young ladies starve themselves, deceiving themselves that they are fat and ugly.

For several years doctors, counselors, psychologists and psychiatrists had worked with Kathy to stop her self-destructive course.

Nothing worked.

Kathy seemed determined to starve herself to death. She was convinced that the doctors would block her success, so she would lie about her diet, would carry weights in her pockets when she stepped onto the doctor's scales ... and steadfastly refused to discuss a terrible secret in her life which she honestly didn't think had anything to do with her problem.

Finally, one day, a doctor told Kathy that her body was suffering irreversible damage and that she was dying.

She panicked.

"I don't want to die," she wailed. "I want to live. I want to live!"

She sought help from a Christian friend.

And it was there, with the help of the Lord, that the reason for her compulsive self-starvation was discovered.

Her own father had sexually abused her from age five until she left home after graduating from high school. Her mother knew what was going on — but instead of intervening, blamed the girl and heaped guilt on her.

Some would respond that incest is not just a modern problem. Bible readers know that it existed thousands of years ago. To what extent it prevailed, we cannot know for sure. It is a hidden problem, something that we've felt free to discuss only in recent years.

In II Samuel, we read of the broken relationship between King David and his son, Amnon. Amnon apparently raped his half-sister, Tamar. It ruined her life and incited her brother, Absolom, to murder Amnon — driving a fatal wedge between David and Absolom.

In another Biblical account, Lot's daughters plotted to become pregnant by their father in order to carry on the family name.

In both of these examples, we can see how a single event affected the lives of family members for generations to come. Would you believe that the descendants of Lot by these incestuous unions are to this day thorns in the side of the Jewish nation?

Sin, no matter how it is rationalized, brings nothing but death.

James 1:15 reads, "Then, after desire has conceived, it gives birth to sin; and sin, when it is full-grown, gives birth to death."

In our society of incredible personal freedom, we have fallen into every form of free sex.

The sad thing is that even Christians have become calloused toward such commonplace sin.

Let me tell you this:

It matters little whether we have become complacent toward such blatant contradictions to God's standards. I say to you, it is sin.

And the stench of it rises all the way to God's nostrils.

If we do not care enough to rescue these "little ones" that Jesus warned us sternly not to harm, I believe we will have to answer at the judgment seat.

Is there hope for these innocent victims?

Let me share with you the story of a young girl, Sharon, who came to one of our centers for help.

When she walked through the door, it was obvious that a dark cloud of guilt and shame hung over her.

Her high school guidance counselor accompanied her and introduced her to the staff. Immediately, I sensed an impenetrable wall of distrust. It was almost impossible to hold eye contact with her.

We all sat down in an attempt to ease the tension Sharon was feeling. As she looked up, her face was filled with anguish and her eyes were swollen with tears.

"I hate my father," she angrily blurted out.

I knew immediately that Sharon was a victim of incest. I felt pain in my heart as though I had been stabbed.

I'd seen too many of these precious girls all but destroyed emotionally through these "sins of the fathers." We prayed with her and asked God for a miracle.

It would take nothing less.

For several days, we worked intently, trying to build a relationship of trust with Sharon. Then, one evening during church services, the Holy Spirit finally broke through. She began to sob uncontrollably as she asked Jesus to come into her heart. Immediately, the face that had been so overcome with shame began to radiate the joy and peace of Christ. When Sharon said, "I really do love my father now," we knew the miracle we had prayed for had happened.

Forgiveness is the only way to be completely healed of emotional scars such as these.

The moment that Sharon received Christ into her heart, love was born.

And from that love came forgiveness.

Incest victims, I have found, are eaten up with bitterness toward their oppressors. They are never free to be healed until that bitterness is replaced with genuine forgiveness.

But incest — however awful that it is, is not the only curse being handed down generation to generation.

As I sought the Lord, I also observed two deadly extremes of parenting.

On the one hand, I witnessed tragic neglect — parents laden with emotional distress and so thoroughly engrossed in their own problems that the kids were left alone to raise themselves.

Part of that group would be the economic and career climbers where both parents work, and where children become "latch key" kids returning home from school to empty houses — where they can watch the cable TV pornography channel, sample the liquor cabinet, try out drugs and pursue their young whims and temptations without adult interference.

A recent Associated Press news article noted that fewer teens have their first sex in the back seats of cars these days. Instead, they experiment at home between 3 p.m. and 6 p.m., before their parents get home from work.

Single-parent homes must be included here as well. Obviously, some parental neglect is unintentional and seemingly unavoidable. Many parents feel they have little choice — especially one-parent homes.

But the fact remains that neglected children, for whatever cause, are left to themselves and experience deep and lasting harm — not the least of which is a sense of rejection.

They may be dearly loved, but absent parents cannot communicate that love — or anything else. We cannot teach our children sound principles that equip them to face the complexities of life if we seldom see them.

What is the result?

I look at the climb of teenage pregnancy.

I look at the growing incidence of youngsters experimenting with perversion and drugs.

I blame parents who let their kids listen to rock music — yes, parents who fail to meet their responsibility to determine what will go into their kids' young minds. I am incredulous at times with parents who ignore the damage that rock music is doing.

And it's not just rock music. Other parents refuse to let their youngsters listen to the Satanism, sex, violence intertwined and defiance of authority in Twisted Sister, Prince, Motley Crue and AC/DC lyrics — **yet** ...

Yet, these same parents take their youngsters to see movies where the most "hilarious" plot devices are:

• grinning pre-teen-agers using profane language — while the movie's recorded "laugh track" roars, as if a filthy-mouthed child is the funniest thing ever imagined;

• unpopular teens finding social acceptance by trying out drugs with their more "cool" peers;

• destruction of property — Are we doing our children a service by howling in laughter with them as escaping bad guys turn traffic into a junkyard?

• "normal" sex — meaning the discovery by the film's youngsters that love is beautiful, and that sex is the answer to everything.

• defiance of authority — If you haven't noticed, movies aimed at youngsters have a recurring theme: that people in authority don't know what they are doing — that kids have to defy them and make the right decisions.

And while I'm on my soapbox, I might as well chide parents who listen to popular country music — paying no attention to its glorification of immorality. No, it may not have pro-drug lyrics — instead it has good-old-boy, everybody's-drinkin' lyrics. And a whole genre of country music is "cheatin' " songs — sympathetic ballads about adultery.

What's the answer?

Pay attention to what the world is piping into your homes and minds — be it rock or *Miami Vice* or defiance of authority or *Love Boat* or occultic Saturday morning cartoons.

Look at today's alarming epidemic of teenage suicides. The media bombards us with news of children ending lives that have barely begun.

"Why did she do this to me?" wails a bereft mother. "Nobody knows except Julie," the newsman intones somberly.

Is this all fulfillment of the curse?

I believe so.

The parents fail to meet their responsibilities to raise the kids — not just provide for them financially.

And the children suffer.

In the traditional home, when the pressures of life become overwhelming to a child, the parents sense the withdrawal or temperament change. A little adult input follows.

The child feels loved and goes on to the next crisis. And Mom or Dad will be there again to pick up the pieces, dry the tears and assure the youngster that all is well in the world.

It's The Kids Who Suffer

But when the parents are gone ... the child has no one.

And the world becomes a truly dark and fearsome place.

As I sought the Lord about this ancient curse, I saw another extreme, too.

That would be parents who completely alter their lives and place their children center stage in every consideration — beginning at birth.

They change their entire lifestyles to accommodate any little whim of the child. Multiply that by two, three, or four children, and you see parents frantically scrambling to meet conflicting schedules.

Little semblance of real family life survives. It is just a mad race of meeting schedules, athletic practices and deadlines — and of parents scurrying to obey their little monarchs' desires of the moment.

No wonder children, as well as adults, are developing ulcers.

Neither extreme lays a secure foundation for a child's future.

Are there answers?

Can we break the curse?

Yes.

6

How Can I Break the Curse?

Kids need parents who are stable. They need parents who know the Lord.

They need parents who are willing to obey God. They need parents who will intercede fervently and daily before the Lord for those kids.

They need parents who are available when the storms of life come crashing down on their inexperienced heads.

The most worthwhile investment parents can ever make is to do everything within their power to insure a strong, godly home foundation. This alone provides the breeding ground for emotionally, mentally, and spiritually strong adults of the future.

And in one way, this breaks the curse.

How?

A generation knows the Lord, is secure in his love and the love of the parents — and has a base on which to build the next generation.

Now that my children are growing older, I am beginning to see a distinct relationship between the Old Testament "sins of the fathers" warning and the New Testament declaration that whatever you sow, you will reap.

School is a good example of that Scriptural law. I wish I had known that what I put into my studies years ago was exactly what I would carry with me through the rest of my life. I probably wouldn't have exerted more effort had someone warned me, but I certainly wish I had "sown" more seeds of learning when I had the opportunity.

The same is true spiritually.

If we fail as parents to heed God's Word, if we refuse to allow him to deal with unruly areas of our lives and continue to walk in disobedience, our children imitate us and find themselves battling with the same sins when they become adults.

Thus, parents' sins are visited upon the children.

Yes, children suffer terribly at the hand of ungodly, unrepentant adults, but those adults suffer even worse, I believe.

Often, they were victims of the same abuse they are now visiting upon the next generation.

On the last night of a crusade in Los Angeles, a very well-dressed and obviously well-educated woman came to me.

"I've got to talk to you," she wept. "I've just got to talk to someone. This thing is killing me, absolutely killing me."

What was her problem?

I discovered that she was at the altar because of her 8-year-old son. The little boy was standing beside her, his eyes anxious and fearful.

"I am a Christian," the woman blurted, "but for five years I have been abusing my son. I have beaten him, locked him in a closet, kept food from him and tied him to the bed. I know I am destroying him, but I can't help it. I need deliverance."

I knelt down and pulled the little boy close to me.

Then, I prayed for them both.

When I was finished, the child looked up at his mother and said, "I forgive you, Mom. I love you. I don't know why you did this to me, but I love you. I always have loved you."

Yes, that little boy had always loved his mother. He had no idea why she did those things to him. But he loved her.

And now he forgave her.

Jesus forgave her, too.

And for the first time, she forgave herself.

The poor mother sobbed and sobbed as she prayed. She confessed her sin openly and asked God for deliverance and healing.

And she was set free.

Forgiveness.

How can I, too, neglect my own daughters by spending so much time on the road?

How I have wrestled with that dilemma — feeling God's call to evangelism, yet knowing that at home Gloria was having to serve as both mother and father.

"Laura," I asked one of my daughters one afternoon, "how do you feel about your daddy being a preacher?"

She and I were having lunch out together. I wanted to spend several hours talking with her — particularly since she had reminded me that I hadn't been taking very much time out with her.

She pondered my question very seriously — much more seriously than I would have expected.

"Daddy," she answered slowly — and obviously a bit painfully, "your life is part of my life and, well, you choose to be in the ministry.

"So," she said, "it's my ministry, too. It's our ministry. If you suffer, I suffer. Since I was little, Mom has taught me to pray for you when you're on the road — and she has explained to me the importance of your role. I accept it and I back you up 100 percent because through all of this, we are still close as a family. Regardless of our differences, we still have Christ.

"I understand your ministry and I am proud of the life you live. I accept it as a blessing and with that I am willing to make the sacrifice to pray for you constantly. Your glory is our glory. Your disgrace is our disgrace."

I was truly touched.

Although I make efforts to spend extra time with each of my four girls — taking them one-at-a-time on ministry trips with me so that we can have special times together ... yet, that still hadn't made up for the times that they had needed Daddy to be at home — instead of being out obeying the Lord's call.

Yes, Laura had missed me. Yes, she had resented my absences throughout her childhood. But through Jesus, she understood and forgave. And through prayer, she was with me on the road.

I am a truly fortunate man to have such a daughter.

Forgiveness.

It sounds too simple to work.

But it does.

Forgiveness can break the curse of the generations.

But it must be ongoing.

Daily.

Seek the Lord as you raise your kids.

Walk in faith.

Abide in the Lord's presence. Immerse yourself in his word.

And seek forgiveness as you make mistakes. Seek it from your kids.

Seek it from the Lord.

And you will break the curse.

The Holy Ghost Hospital

7

I'm About to Crack Up

I love taking Jesus to Latin America. There are lots of hurting people there — people who need Jesus.

I can preach with power in my native Spanish.

And Latins aren't intimidated like most of us in the United States.

When they feel the power of the Lord, they jump up and show it — the men particularly. I'd say that 70 percent of those who come to the Lord in our Latin American crusades are men — big, macho guys who kneel before their Creator, weeping openly, begging for his forgiveness and leaping up in joy and power as he touches them, forgives them and fills them with his presence.

But Satan's deceit is very great in Latin America, too. In the South American country of Paraguay once, 2,000 witches were preaching and praying against us as we began a crusade in the capital of Asuncion. Yet ... the

Christians of Paraguay were praying, too —
with great faith for a national revival.

During the crusade — on one night in
particular — 45,000 people gathered in the
national stadium. The movie, *The Cross and
the Switchblade* had been on national TV three
times, so, we had a lot of interest.

But that night, it was as if there was an evil
cloud over the place.

I could feel the power of Satan trying to
choke us. I turned to one of my Paraguayan
brothers. "We gotta pray," I whispered to him.
"That cloud is Lucifer — the power of death."
People on the stage and behind it began to seek
the Lord's help.

And the evil broke. In the presence of the
faith of God's people, Satan must retreat.

The cloud parted.

The Lord allowed me to speak with power
and authority. About 45 minutes into the
service, I opened the altar and more than 5,000
people began streaming down the aisles, coming to the Lord.

Well, Satan didn't like that.

He launched a counterattack.

We suddenly had more than 250 Satanists
running all over the place — screaming,
cursing, disrupting, generally trying to take
over.

So, I again took authority in the name of
Jesus. We prayed for them.

Dramatically, in the midst of that vast crowd, they were delivered. They fell, screaming, shaking. Officials of the Paraguayan national Red Cross wanted to take them to the hospital.

I told them "Don't touch them." They were OK. Jesus had delivered them. They didn't need man's medical treatment.

They had been to the Holy Ghost Hospital.

Over the next five days, 21,000 people came to know Jesus. Many required treatment at the Holy Ghost Hospital.

I've been there, too. What is it?

Remember the old-time country hospital? Regardless of one's ability to pay, or ethnic background, or station in life — if anyone was ill, injured or dying, the hospital was the one place to be counted upon to open its doors for healing. Neither modern hospitals nor churches, as a whole, retain such a policy today. We read and watch television documentaries about people who died because a hospital refused to take them in.

Just yesterday I heard on the news about an infant who needed a liver transplant to live. But somehow, the word didn't get out nationwide.

Only after the parents made an emotional appeal to the White House did First Lady Nancy Reagan use her influence to draw attention to the situation — and pledge to send Air

Force One to transport a donor liver to the dying child.

Within hours one was found ...

But it was too late. The baby died.

"If only all this could have happened 24 hours earlier," the transplant surgeon told a news conference.

But so many times help doesn't come at all.

My good friend Marvin Gorman, the pastor of a large church in New Orleans, has told of a dream he had that shook up his whole ministry. In his dream, he was given a tour of a beautiful, glistening hospital. The floors gleamed — spotless. The very latest in electronic equipment waited in white, sparkling labs. Extremely professional, immaculately dressed staff members scurried about efficiently. Nurses filed reports, sorted trays of medicines and consulted with supervisors.

White-jacketed doctors studied clipboards and talked with one another in learned tones — discussing the nobility of medicine and latest developments in healing the sick.

But there was something strange about the hospital.

It had no patients. The beds were empty.

As Gorman pondered this oddity, things changed abruptly   as they do in dreams.

Suddenly the wide halls were filled with the bloody, the sick and injured. Ambulances screamed up to the spotless emergency room, discharging dirty, wounded, weeping people.

Shocked, the hospital staff stood back from the new arrivals. They backed away from all the torn flesh and disease. With righteous authority, doctors began ordering the patients out — rebuking them for defacing the hospital with their sickness and contagion and blood.

These sick people had no respect for the place of healing, the physicians muttered as the place cleared out — and once again the hospital was quiet.

Gorman says he awoke and fell to his knees.

"Forgive us, Lord," he pleaded — pledging then and there that his congregation would rise to the needs all around. "The church today has been no better than the religious leaders of your day."

Indeed, Jesus rebuked the Pharisees and High Priests, calling them whitewashed sepulchers — sparkling tombs, impressive on the outside, yet filled with dusty bones on the inside.

The Lord chose to take his ministry to the sick, the outcast, the unwanted. He fellowshiped with illiterate fishermen, prostitutes and hated tax collectors — collaborators with the Romans.

So, how do we dare to ignore his example?

Believers, too, perish today because the church will not reach out and minister at a times when they are down.

The church has forgotten it was established to be a "Holy Ghost Hospital" where spiritual war casualties can enter and believers will be standing by ready to lie down and give their blood if necessary — to make a transfusion into the lives of the hurting.

But increasingly, a great many of the hurting are denied entrance — or shunned when they do dare to enter uninvited.

Why?

Why?

Why?

Don't Shoot, I'm Already Wounded! cried the title of a book published a few years ago.

The story was of a woman whose life had been drastically transformed when she found Jesus Christ as her savior. She began a fruitful ministry, traveling all over the world as a much sought-after speaker.

Then tragedy struck.

Her husband of many years divorced her.

She was shattered.

But worse than that, doors of ministry slammed shut. Fellowship opportunities dwindled.

"The church," it has been stated, "is the only army that shoots its wounded."

When I ponder that statement, my heart is crushed beneath the staggering truth of it. What, in heaven's name, causes redeemed brethren to turn on each other with such vengeance?

Why do we devour our weakened, wounded comrades with gossip, pointed fingers, cold shoulders and whispered accusations?

"Almost every time I worked up the courage to climb out, I found another Christian's foot on my throat," bemoaned a woman as she recounted to me her struggle to overcome years of wasted youth.

Today she is serving the Lord in a fruitful music ministry, but no thanks to fellow Christians who virtually dared her to rise above her self-created gutter.

What is the church's problem?

Instead of existing to help the hurting, fallen soldiers of the cross, the church actually seems preoccupied with killing off its wounded.

How many people are totally lost to the cause of Christ because of heartless treatment within the body of Christ?

"At a time when I was desperate for help," we often hear, "no one reached out to me. All they did was criticize. Why should I waste my time in such a hypocritical institution? I find more compassion at the local bar."

What a stinging indictment!

We must be able to say to the hurting, "I am here to help you. I am here to give you my strength. No one needs to know what has happened. I will keep it confidential. It's true that what you did was wrong, but I refuse to judge you because I am just like you — 'only a sinner, saved by grace.' "

Do you remember the old television sitcom, "M*A*S*H"? Setting aside problems concerning the questionable moral value of that series, consider what happened in each episode when wounded soldiers were heard helicoptering in.

"Incoming wounded!" barked the camp's loudspeakers. There was instant abandonment of everyday activities, a mad scramble, shouting, and a rush to administer healing before life ebbed away.

Why can't we behave in the same way?

The church is engaged in a fearsome war.

The forces of hell stand arrayed against us. God tells us our true enemy, Satan, is like a roaring lion waiting to devour us. We all are deceived by this enemy more than we care to admit and we can't help but be wounded from time to time.

Yes, of course, we can go to the Lord.

His own Holy Ghost Hospital operates well without our involvement. But many of the wounded need a human touch. They need to see Jesus through *you*.

The New Testament commands that we not forsake the fellowshiping of one another. This doesn't just mean we should go to church every Sunday.

It means we must get involved, working together with other believers, building spiritual relationships.

There is healing in Christian fellowship.

Satan knows it.

So, he subverts our churches so that there is no fellowship, just criticism and gossip and political games.

As Satan laughs with glee, Christians waste their energies by fighting the wrong enemy — one another!

Satan knows that a house divided falls.

Wherever I travel and preach in crusades, I see the same thing.

North Ireland is a classic example. Many churches and supposed religious organizations are armed camps with Protestants and Catholics plotting murder, arson, vandalism, intimidation and terrorism. Church leaders denounce fellow Christians and condone bombings, ambushes and assassination.

I know of another country where the Christians currently are fighting like cats and dogs — taking their theological nitpicking out before non-Christians on the radio and television airwaves.

As they fight one another, denouncing one another and slandering the brotherhood, the major result is the public ridicule of Christ — by Christians demonstrating that love does not work and that forgiveness cannot be practiced.

Satan howls with mirth.

In America, to the average onlooker, the religious scene today appears to be a great number of enemy camps scrambling to persuade people to come under their label. All who do not conform to the standards and Scriptural interpretations of each label come under fire.

Conservatives are fighting liberals, fundamentalists are after pentecostals, the non-denominationalists are divided into premillenialists and post-millenialists, and everyone disagrees loudly with everyone else.

Take a look at the Saturday religious section in your local newspaper. Study the church ads carefully, and you can quickly detect the individual rivalries.

If the sermon titles don't clue you in, the stated church policies will. We quickly build walls designed to keep the inside people in and the outside people out. We are deluded into thinking that the outside people are the enemy as we level our verbal guns at them.

I am reminded of an incident that took place in the early 1800's.

The British army marched to a French-occupied city. The plan was to surround the city, move in and attack. Arriving earlier than they had planned, the soldiers readied themselves for battle and began to wait for the appointed hour. With nothing to do, however, the men decided to stage a "victory celebration" and began to drink.

A Catholic church stood nearby with a courtyard full of life-size "saints" — St. Matthew, St. Peter, St. Timothy, St. Paul, and even St. Mary.

In their drunkenness, the celebrating soldiers began shooting at the marble figures. One after another, they aimed their guns at the lifelike statues and howled with glee as the stone figures tumbled.

But imagine their surprise when the French army mustered troops and surrounded the attackers. The British soldiers had given away their positions and used all their ammunition "shooting the saints."

Not a bullet was left to use against the real enemy.

Who is our enemy?

Certainly not the saints, even if they happen to be behind someone else's wall rather than our own.

Satan and all his hosts comprise our true enemy and he is after us. God said, "Your enemy, the devil, prowls around like a roaring lion looking for someone to devour. Resist him ..." (I Peter 5:8).

Did you know that there are more than 27,000 witches in America praying continually for demons to penetrate every Gospel-preaching church?

That's right. Paraguay isn't the only foothold of Satanism. It is increasingly strong on America's West Coast — and even in the "Bible Belt" of the Midwest.

Specifically, I am told, American Satan worshipers are praying that ministers will fall, families be divided, and Christians will be a disgrace to their communities and to Jesus.

That's the real enemy at work.

Not our brothers in other denominations.

What was Jesus trying to say when he kept praying, "that they all may be one?"

If he meant that he desires all his followers, all born-again believers, to be unified in heart and purpose, I must say it looks hopeless — if it's left up to us bickering humans.

If he didn't mean that, what then was he trying to get across?

Frankly, I am bewildered when I view at close range the church worldwide.

What I see, for the most part, is church groups fighting each other because of differences in theology — often miniscule.

While the battle rages, the lost and wounded sit huddled in their emptiness and wonder where to turn.

Certainly, Satan whispers in their ears, they can't find answers in these religious battlefields:

That would be like sending an exhausted, bullet-ridden soldier off to a brand-new war where everybody shoots everybody else — **regardless of uniform.**

No wonder Jesus emphasized his longing that we all be one.

He knew what would happen if we refused to love and serve each other.

Becoming one will force us to lay aside all our petty differences so that the Church might display Christ's love.

What about denominations?

Jesus never planned for his people to be separated by such manmade walls.

It was his desire to build one church. If God has called you to be a part of a certain denomination, that is fine, but don't attack those whom God has not called to be there with you.

Am I saying we should instantly abolish denominational structure?

No.

I can, however, emphatically assert that the fighting, the bitterness, the finger-pointing and the refusal to cooperate with each other on any issue, and the general spirit of competitiveness cannot possibly be pleasing to the Saviour who earnestly prayed to His Father in heaven "that they may be one even as we are one."

Four times Jesus repeated this plea.

The reason for this oneness, He stated, was so that the world might believe that the Father had sent His Son.

Now if Christian unity proves to the world that Jesus Christ is the Son of God, the absence of unity gives the opposite message. I live in Colorado Springs, a city boasting more than the usual number of large Christian organizations. We are blessed with Christian leadership all over our community.

But I am told by evangelists that it is next to impossible to find enough cooperating churches to organize any city-wide evangelistic effort.

A noted evangelist recently almost canceled his scheduled crusade here for lack of local church support.

Why didn't the churches here work together for a city-wide outreach? They couldn't agree on the minor issues.

Is Colorado Springs an isolated example?

Certainly not.

Are the perishing souls of men and women not incentive enough to forget our differences and go after them? Perhaps the careless way the church treats its fallen members is an outgrowth of this strong denominational structure that builds walls instead of bridges.

And if a lack of unity determines the world's estimate of the validity of Christianity, then our hostility towards Christians overcome by sin may be a large part of why we are held in such disrepute.

I don't condone sin, but I say that we must love sinners. All of us are candidates to sin — even though we cannot let sin reign and control us as in the past before we knew Christ.

Nevertheless, when a brother falls, the Bible doesn't instruct you to shun him or kick him.

We're to lift one another up.

Sure, if he refuses to stop sinning, we are given guidelines for removing him or her from leadership — and then from fellowship. But such are extreme circumstances.

Yet, we invoke these instructions almost in glee — as if delighting that we can cast our spiritual rivals into outer darkness.

And all the world sees is hypocrisy and inconsistency.

We preach love ... and practice *hate*.

It need not be so.

While on a recent crusade in a Latin American country, a man and his wife came forward during a service seeking healing and deliverance. Later I was invited to dinner in their home and discovered he was an outstanding medical doctor. A brilliant man with a devoted wife and lovely family. After dinner, my host drew me aside and poured out his heart to me.

I couldn't believe the nightmare this family was going through.

Some of the members of his church had been jealous of his success and financial security.

He was a respected leader in the church and he had been witnessing to professional people and leading them to Christ. The presence of these professionals threatened a few of the common folk. Eventually someone began whispering that the doctor was involved in moral sin.

This idea was so preposterous even to his wife that they paid little attention, supposing no one would believe such an unfounded lie. The whispering grew, suspicion mounted, and the church became sharply divided on the issue.

Almost before he knew it, this innocent man became the victim of violent accusations. Even the pastor joined the assailants and instead of privately going to counsel with the accused, he used his pulpit to lash out.

It became necessary for the family to leave the church, and even though the accusations were totally without support, the man's self-image was destroyed. As he poured out his story, he broke down and wept like a little child.

I quickly detected that all he needed was someone to love him.

Someone who would bind up his bleeding wounds, lead him to forgiveness towards his enemies, pray with him, and assure him of his worth in God's eyes.

That's all I did, but that was exactly what he needed to get a fresh start.

That's the Holy Ghost Hospital in action. The Lord healed this Christian doctor's deep hurts. But first, a human brother had to extend Christian love.

A poignant news story from California recently stirred us with compassion. A 14-year-old girl, Donna Ashlock, was afflicted with a serious heart ailment and desperately needed a heart transplant to survive.

Her 15-year-old neighbor, Felipe Garza, had a deep teenage crush on her and told his mother, "When I die, I want to give her my heart." No one quite understood what he was saying.

Apparently, he had an intuition of his death, for less than a week later, a blood vessel burst in his brain and he died.

His heart was transplanted immediately to the girl he loved from a distance.

Today, she is in excellent health because of his sacrifice. What better illustration of what the church needs today? If we could give our hearts, our lifeblood, to weak and ailing believers, the whole body could be healthier as a result. Not once, but many times, a strange event has occurred at my crusades.

It involves married couples who have either separated or divorced. Unknown to either of them, both attend a service. With thousands of people there, they do not see each other.

At the end of the sermon as I issue the challenge to come follow Jesus, both come forward from opposite corners of the stadium, never knowing until much later what has happened. These estranged partners who separately are seeking forgiveness and restoration are brought together at the feet of Jesus in the same meeting.

What miracles of restoration could happen if disgruntled believers would be willing to bury petty differences and come together on this one issue — to "bind up the brokenhearted, proclaim freedom for the captives, release the prisoners ... and comfort all who mourn." (Luke 4:18)

And consider the following: "We who are strong ought to bear with the failings of the weak and not to please ourselves" (Romans 5:1); "If someone is caught in a sin, you who are spiritual should restore him gently" (Galatians 6:1); and "Be kind and compassionate to one another, forgiving each

other, just as in Christ God forgave you,"
Ephesians 4:32.

We see today so many pastors, evangelists,
and teachers that are self-acclaimed prophets.
The truth of their message is sometimes
obscured by an overabundance of judgment.

They are prophets of doom spreading
nothing but negativity and pessimism. They
preach the law — as if they have forgotten that
we live under grace. They use a one-edged
sword that cuts the ear so severely the person
listening cannot hear the real message for the
blood and pain.

It is as if they don't realize that we no
longer live under the law — but under grace!
So, why do they preach legalism and death?
The law goes after your lungs — and steals
your life's breath. But grace goes after your
heart — and gives life and breath.

Can such pastors and evangelists have lost
their vision? Jesus told Peter to "feed my sheep"
not herd them with electric cattle prods!

Proverbs 16:6 says, "By mercy and truth sin
is purged ..." So we see, it takes both mercy and
truth to get sin out of someone's life. Not
condemnation or judgment.

A doctor will know how to remove cancer,
but if he starts cutting without first admin-
istering anesthesia, the pain will kill the
patient during the process which should have
brought healing.

Jesus uses a two-edged sword: one edge cuts — the other edge heals.

We remember Peter cutting off a soldier's ear in the Garden of Gethsemane. Jesus, with gentleness, restored the severed ear. Healing was manifested and the soldier could hear what Jesus was saying.

It is true our Lord is a God of judgment, but the circumstances and situations in our lives today are going to force us into a confrontation with the convicting power of the Holy Spirit.

At that point, we have the choice to repent or rebel.

When we repent, the Holy Spirit pours the oil of healing and restoration on our wounds.

What should a hospital do?

A registered nurse spoke with me about the hospital where she works. "When a person comes into our hospital, it is because they need help. We give them help. We tend to their needs, for example, a broken arm — but we also consider the total being.

"If a man with a broken arm is worried about his wallet and how he is going to find work and feed his family, his arm will not heal quickly. Worry is sometimes worse than the injury itself.

"A drug addict may overdose," she continued. "But even though he may go out on the streets and do it again, we try to save his life and get him healthy. When the ambulance brings the same man in again, we are there with life-saving equipment ready to save his life once more. No matter how many times a person needs help, we never turn them away."

Churches don't always adhere to such policies. We throw up our hands when a repeat offender comes in again bruised and mangled.

We berate them and cast them from fellowship — without following the guidelines penned by the Apostle Paul. He never said that we are to abandon the weak Christian who is honestly trying to find a way out of his or her personal quagmire.

Certainly such people may have to be put aside in terms of leadership.

But excommunication has strict rules.

Too often, I fear, the church's outlook on helping repeat offenders becomes conditional.

"How influential is that person?"

"Would he or she be able to contribute to the building fund?"

"Would we be embarrassed in our fine institution to have that kind of person?"

We pray for a hurting person, but then turn around and wound him even deeper through criticism and gossip. If a weak brother or sister falls again, our actions seem to say, "No, we can't help you. You've had your chance. We can't be wasting our time on people who don't want to get well."

Paul said that the Lord gave us authority "for building you up rather than pulling you down ..." (2 Corinthians 10:8).

That is what the church needs today — to build up and quit tearing down. To be a "Holy Ghost Hospital" for the healing, the rescuing, the building up of God's people.

We must be a people who strengthen, encourage, and comfort one another. And above all — quit criticizing your brothers.

Let me show you exactly what such criticism can do.

8

The Holy Ghost Hospital

"A heart attack last year was the greatest thing that ever happened to me," said the man with whom I had struck up a conversation on a flight from Colorado Springs to London, England.

I didn't believe I had heard him correctly. A heart attack had been the greatest thing to happen to him?

"Yes, that's exactly what I said. And I really mean it." He began to explain that as a busy executive of a large corporation, he found himself speeding through life at a breakneck pace. Facing daily business pressures in the office, he flew all over the country attending meetings, speaking at seminars, settling employee disputes and coping with the stress of each individual situation. Finally it became more than he could handle. Something had to give. It turned out to be his heart.

He hovered between life and death for days. As he recovered, he found his whole life had ground to a halt. Daily pressures had melted away and he saw things in clear perspective for the first time in years.

"I am a completely changed person," he told me proudly. "I've learned to be happy with things just as they are, and I assure you, I will never again place myself in a situation where stress is the dominant factor. Frankly, I can't if I want to continue living."

Stress is a killer.

But recovery can be so much harder when the stress comes not from the enemy — but from other Christians.

Let me tell you about two friends of mine, Jan and Paul, who decided to sit down and see what their kids were watching on children's TV.

What they saw deeply alarmed them. From the Saturday morning cartoons right on through the prime-time shows, they realized that a blast of filth had defiantly shoved its way into their Christian home.

Furthermore, their kids were addicted to it. Jan and Paul gawked in disbelief at the blatant witchcraft, deadly violence and a steady stream of sex — all of it captivating their youngsters' impressionable minds.

Upon questioning other parents, they realized that few adults bothered to get out of bed on Saturday mornings to monitor what the children were watching. Fewer still wanted to weather their kids' protests when restrictions were placed on what could or couldn't be watched.

When my friends wanted to talk about the influence on Christian adults of the networks' evening family offerings, fellow Christians just shrugged off the occult messages being offered in such then-popular shows as *Bewitched* and *I Dream of Jeanie,* the sexual mockery of *Love American Style* and *Rowan & Martin's Laugh-in* and the constant message on detective and police dramas that violence and death are fine when used for the right cause.

Bear in mind this was several years ago — long before the blatant decadence of *Miami Vice, Three's Company* or *Love Boat,* the sex and violence of rock music's M-tv, before X-rated cable TV was being piped into homes, before "sensitive docu-dramas" were illustrating the joys of lesbianism and homosexuality — and long before today's dark and violent cartoons featured *Dungeons & Dragons, He-Man, Ashera, Voltron* and so forth.

Jan and Paul became alarmed. They couldn't help but see why the moral erosion of American youth had turned into a landslide. They could see reasons for what was happening to well-trained, church-attending kids reared in solid Christian homes.

TV had infiltrated the church's homes, sneaking around moral barriers — importing the devil's death and sin into Christian living rooms.

Something had to be done, Jan and Paul decided.

It was right there that God spoke to them. He didn't tell them to erect impressive buildings or to spend inordinate amounts of money, or to secure the help of big name entertainers.

He just told Jan and Paul Crouch to build a TV station where decent programs and the message of the Gospel could flow.

That became their vision.

The Crouches knew it wouldn't be easy, but they certainly did expect Christians to understand the importance of their task.

Surely God's people wanted to clean up the airways, particularly into their own homes. Such people would support this lofty effort.

Did Christian forces join together to help the Crouches build what was to become Trinity Broadcasting Network? Incredibly, no.

Opposition screamed at them, jealousy reared its ugly head, and a complacent "we'll just wait and see if this pans out" attitude delayed many interested people from investing sorely needed funds.

"It's too Hollywoodish," some complained.

"Not Hollywoodish enough," said others.

"It's clearly of the devil," still others moaned.

Some of Jan and Paul's most trusted confidants turned against them along with many of the largest churches which they had counted on to be staunch supporters.

For a time it seemed that no one caught their vision.

As opposition mounted, Jan and Paul began to question their leading. Was it really from God? Or had they missed his will somewhere in the confused mess?

What had gone wrong?

Even God seemed silent at the point of their deepest need. Everything they touched failed. Maybe they had been crazy to undertake such an impossible project.

"Both Paul and I were in great distress, but it affected me differently," Jan remembers. "I slipped into deep mental depression. I was like a zombie. All of my energy was gone, I couldn't think clearly, and I knew my emotions were completely out of control. Literally, I was paralyzed with fear and pain — afraid I was losing my vision, my inspiration, my husband, my family. All I could do was just sit and cry uncontrollably. If anyone had told me in the beginning that this could have happened, I'd have laughed. I probably would have assured them that such a thing never could happen to Christians — especially me.

"I'm really strong in the Lord, you know. But I was so wrong. I even contemplated suicide. Often during those days I walked by the ocean near our home wondering how to make my death look like an accident. I thought about wading into the water and just walking until I was embraced in the arms of the angel of death."

How often did she have these destructive thoughts?

"All the time. All the time. The stress I experienced simply wiped me out. I couldn't take care of my children or my house. I couldn't even cook. My life seemed so useless that I kept thinking how much better off everyone would be without me."

Only an act of God kept her from taking her life, she says. Not the intervention of a caring Christian — but the direct intercession of our Lord God.

"It was a miracle that rescued me from my dreams of death," she remembers. "An absolute miracle. No one will ever convince me otherwise. One day when I had skidded to the lowest point of my existence, I was lying in bed unable to move or think. My poor little children had to take care of themselves. Suddenly I became conscious of a scorching smell. Something in the kitchen was burning. But I didn't move. Subconsciously I knew the children must be trying to fix something to eat, although they were too young to know how to cook. However, it really didn't matter to me at this point.

Even if the house burned down, that was all right. Then my misery would end.

"As I lay there immersed with longing to escape, quite suddenly an angel of death appeared. How I knew that's what he was, I really can't tell you.

"I had slipped so deeply into depression that I was practically comatose. But still I knew who that angel was. He had come for me. I knew this.

"The thought startled me.

"I clearly saw in that moment that what was happening was not in the physical realm at all.

"Then God showed me the tragic, irreversible consequences of my death wish. It was almost as if he would grant my wish if I persisted, but that I would never know his forgiveness or the realization of his plans for my life.

"It was awesome. You understand I am not trying to explain all of this theologically — I am simply recounting what happened.

"You can't even imagine how utterly helpless I was.

"The incredible thing is that when I realized my decision to live or die was for all eternity, deep within me arose a faint desire to live.

"It was very faint, but enough to turn the tide of events. The angel of death retreated.

"While I pulled out of the depths of depression, still I was not happy," Jan remembers. "Now I didn't want to die, but living wasn't great either. Everything I did seemed mechanical — going through motions. Quality of life was next to rock bottom.

"But God did a wonderful thing for me. It came by way of another dream. In it I was walking on the beach alongside the same ocean where I had walked so often before and plotted death. But this time I felt an inexplicable peace.

"I kept on walking, and I saw a crowd of people ahead. They were in a circle and appeared to be gathered around a person in the center. I paused awhile to take in the scene before me. Then I noticed a large tree growing nearby, and some of the people ambled over and sat under the tree. Soon everyone in that circle was sitting under the tree.

"Then I moved closer and saw that all the people were laughing and enjoying themselves. When finally I could spot the center of their attention, I recognized Jesus.

"There he was in the midst of the gathered people.

"He was smiling and laughing with them. I couldn't believe what I saw.

"Jesus was actually enjoying the companionship of his people. Jesus had been teaching, but now he was sitting and fellowshiping.

He lifted his head in a gentle gesture, smiling and laughing with his friends.

"Suddenly I experienced a new Jesus. He was a friend I could enjoy. I could laugh with him. I could relax in his presence.

"I woke up from the dream laughing, and I felt the Holy Spirit pervading my whole room. Although I couldn't have explained it, I knew it was a new beginning for me. Joy returned to my spirit, and eventually God's inner healing restored me to wholeness again."

God's Holy Ghost Hospital certainly has more stunning results against stress than any puny human psychology, psychoanalysis or psychotherapy.

But what a pity that the worst stress that had driven Jan to the edge of sanity was because of the faithlessness and back-stabbing of fellow Christians!

Stress today constitutes a major dilemma for all of us. When we work too much, let our spiritual guard down, or if we allow ourselves to continually fret about situations, we become vulnerable. But when the attack is joined by fellow Christians, it can become just too much.

"Stress is eating me up, and I know it. I've got to find some way to deal with stress in my life," a young woman, an outstanding children's worker in her church, recently told me. Especially in Christian education, everybody today has an opinion on how things should be done — how the children are being taught too little of this or too much of that.

What a shame! Consider how much energy and creativity could go into improving the program instead! But so many fellow Christians seem content to spend their time taking potshots at each other and becoming envious of those on the front lines of the battle.

When I do counseling in my crusades and even in ordinary social life, stress stares at me constantly. Before I know it, I catch myself fretting and stewing inwardly with the daily grind of problems.

The complex intermeshing of home, office, and travel becomes more than I can balance, and suddenly I am like that young woman — with stress eating at my vitals, without my even realizing it.

What, exactly, is this stress? How should it be treated in the church's Holy Ghost Hospital?

How can the Christian fight stress — particularly unnecessary tension caused by the crass criticism of his brethren?

9

How Can I Survive?

Trust in the Lord.

Keep your eyes on Jesus, not men.

Fellow humans will always let you down — particularly if you are attempting to seek their constant applause.

Seek the Lord daily in a quiet time.

Make a habit of that.

John Wesley once had commented that he spent one and two hours a day alone in prayer and Bible reading.

"How can you dare?" exclaimed one of his disciples who knew Wesley's hectic daily schedule.

"How can I dare not?" rebutted the old theologian. His strength was in the Lord — not in the plaudits of men.

"The Lord loves the just and will not forsake his faithful ones. They will be protected forever," God promises us in Psalm 37:40.

"I will contend with those who contend with you," he warns in Isaiah 49:25.

"Suffering produces perseverance; perseverance, character; character, hope," he promises in Romans 5:3-4.

And in 1 Peter 3:14, he notes:

"The God of all grace, who called you to his eternal glory in Christ, after you have suffered a little while, will himself restore you and make you strong, firm and steadfast."

Attitude, then, becomes a decisive consideration.

When my attitude is under God's control, criticism and other stressful circumstances can't shake me.

A good attitude, I am discovering, comes from one source only — God.

Daily reading God's Word, daily taking time to pray, and daily turning those spiritual exercises into obedience provide my key to a great attitude.

Walking in obedience to his slightest direction creates an inner joy that cannot be explained.

It is then that God surprises me with the most unusual evidences of His love and care.

Don't neglect fellowship — even if you have been burned by callous fellow believers.

"May the Lord make your love increase and overflow for each other and for everyone else," says 1 Thessalonians 3:12.

"Now that you have purified yourselves by obeying the truth so that you have sincere love for your brothers, love one another deeply, from the heart," admonishes 1 Peter 1:22.

God will be faithful to your obedience.

Your stress will decrease.

"Stress is the rate of wear and tear on the body," said the late Dr. Hans Selye, father of stress research. Others conclude that stress refers to any external stimulus that causes the wear and tear, or the damage inside resulting from it.

If you think that's confusing, think about one researcher's statement summing up the problem in this way: "Stress, in addition to being itself, and the result of itself, is also the cause of itself."

And what is stressful for one person is nothing special at all for another.

"It is a sorry sign of our times that the three best-selling drugs in this country are an ulcer medication (Tagamet), a hypertension drug (Inderal), and a tranquilizer (Valium)," *Time* magazine reports.

Nobody is exempt from this dissipator of vitality and productivity, least of all evangelists, ministers, church workers, and Christians everywhere.

"Two-thirds of the office visits to family doctors come by way of stress-related symptoms," reports the American Academy of Family Physicians.

Meanwhile, industry pays a high price for absenteeism and loss of production.

The total amount of time lost amounts to between $50 and $75 billion annually. Just living in the complicated society of 20th Century America seems to produce enough friction to electrically power a large city.

"While stress might once have taken the form of an occasional calamity, it is now a chronic, relentless, psychological situation," writes Dr. Paul Rosch, Director of the American Institute of Stress. He says today's pressures have created a breed of thrill-seekers who, often to their detriment, prefer excitement over tranquility.

Life in the fast-lane becomes a dangerous habit for them.

"Sky-divers get hooked on the jump, and executives purposely arrive at the airport at the last possible minute. People today have become addicted to their own adrenalin secretions."

And some of us thought drugs, alcohol and sex constituted the world's greatest hang-ups!

Most of the time stress only concerns us when it relates to us personally. It can happen to any of us.

We get tied up in knots just because of the things we think about, let alone the complicated circumstances today's living produces.

What bothers me might not bother you.

But if you get in my way, I can't guarantee that it won't bother you also.

Personally, I would die if I had to sit in the confinement of a space capsule for a prolonged period.

But consider Astronaut Jim Irwin, my friend, neighbor, and fellow evangelist.

He just saw it as a job and went about it in a businesslike manner.

Consider the natural occurrence of a snowstorm.

• To the tense driver with visions of sliding off the road or into another vehicle, snow-packed roads become sources of torturous stress.

• To the skier, on the other hand, falling snow is an unexpected delight.

A year or so after Jan Crouch's healing, she and Paul took a trip to Israel and were walking along the shore of the Sea of Galilee.

They were walking hand in hand, when suddenly Jan looked ahead and her attention was drawn to an astounding sight.

"You won't believe it," she says.

"What I saw was the exact tree of my dream. There is no mistaking it. I had looked so carefully at it in my dream that I actually memorized the contour. It was my tree all right."

I don't doubt Jan's word.

Such a transformation from death to life had occurred in her that all I could do was marvel.

Such are the mighty ways of the Holy Ghost Hospital.

With God, even stress becomes not all bad.

As with the executive with the heart attack, as with Jan in the depth of depression, good can come from seeming evil.

How?

Receive every circumstance in life as coming directly from God's hand for a precise purpose.

"We do not have a high priest who is unable to sympathize with our weaknesses," the Apostle Paul wrote in Hebrews 4:15-16, "but we have one who has been tempted in every way, just as we are — yet was without sin. Let us then approach the throne of grace with confidence, so that we may receive mercy and find grace to help us in our time of need."

God is faithful.

Today Jan Crouch is one of the most compassionate people I know.

She is especially tender towards children — neglected children, molested children, and rejected children.

The memory of her own rejection by fellow Christians remains fresh — along with her own neglect of her children during her months of depression.

So she reaches out to other hurting people.

It never would have happened if the Lord had not walked with her through the fire.

She would not be a changed person had he not taken her from the valley of the shadow of death ...

Into the comfort and intensive care of his glorious Holy Ghost Hospital.

IV

Pregnant By The Holy Spirit

10

Dave

David Wilkerson surely didn't realize how close I came to killing him.

On a street corner in our Brooklyn slum, he seemingly had shown up out of nowhere wearing country-bumpkin clothes, waving an over-sized Bible and trying to convert my gang to Jesus.

I was sick of his clever words.

I was threatened by his success with my best friend, Israel.

I was sure he was a witch — like my mother and dad.

And I hated him. After Israel announced he was turning his life over to Jesus — and that all of us should, too — I knew it was time to kill this Pennsylvania preacher.

Three of my Mau Maus gang members, Hector, Willie and Albert, and I lounged in my room smoking grass and drinking wine. Casually we played with the knives we carried. Hector toyed with a sawed-off shotgun.

Suddenly Willie blurted, "Nicky, it's time to go after the man."

I knew what he was thinking, but I looked him straight in the eye.

"What are you talking about?" I asked.

"Just what I said. It's time to finish that guy. Do you know what a threat he is to us? He walks on our streets — our turf, like he owns it. He comes from someplace in Pennsylvania and he wants to change us. Change *you*, Nicky. Change everybody."

The marijuana had mellowed me. "Aw, come on, Willie," I laughed. "Nobody can change me. You're crazy!"

"Naw," disagreed Albert. "He's right, Nicky. Willie's right."

"What you're saying is that you want to kill this guy, knowing the police will be after us. Well, there's one thing you've forgotten."

"You're wrong, Nicky," Hector jumped in. "We haven't forgotten anything."

"You shut up, Hector," I yelled. "Let me finish."

Hector ignored me. He continued to talk, waving his sawed-off shotgun like it was some kind of magic wand. "You see this, Nicky? This thing can blow half his body away."

Willie laughed. "Nicky, that guy is out to destroy the gang. He's already got Israel thinking dangerous things."

The sweet smell of marijuana fogged the air. The atmosphere grew tense.

"Wait just a minute," I threatened. "I hate this man more than any of you. If I had the time right now, I'd kill him. But you guys are stupid. If we blow him away and throw him in the Hudson River or in the subway, you're forgetting about Israel. He'll be questioned. He'd have to talk to save himself — but I know him. He wouldn't talk. He'd go down before he'd turn us in."

"Forget about Israel." Hector said.

"Don't you ever say 'forget about Israel'," I shot back at him. "This is a family and we have a code of ethics, you know. That's the reason I joined this gang. That's our strength, and we're brothers no matter what we do."

Hector was not going to give up. "Let's tell Israel about our plan. Then we'll toss a coin, and the one who calls it can blow the man away."

Every muscle of my body tensed. I walked over to the refrigerator and pulled out a beer. I wanted Wilkerson dead. But I was serious about the problem that Israel's friendship with him presented. Israel was our leader and my best friend. We could not betray Israel.

Hector became furious, almost hysterical in his desire for blood.

"Shut up!" I snarled at him. "I want Wilkerson dead, too. But everybody in this building can hear you, and the police know Wilkerson has been coming here for two weeks. The guy is afraid of me, but I'm not afraid of him. Yeah, he's talking to Israel, but Israel is the president of this gang — so what are you going to say, Hector?"

"I don't care," he said with a shrug.

However, I knew Hector too well. He was a vicious guy with no respect or loyalty, even to his own gang. I was aware of his brutality, and I couldn't forget that he had once tied up his uncle and whipped him almost to death.

Afterwards, he had bragged about sending the man to the hospital for weeks.

"Hector, if you dare make a move without our knowing, I'll kill you," I said softly. "I'll break every bone in your body. I'll spill your guts in the streets. I'll do it even if it kills me."

We stared at each other.

"Tomorrow," I said, "I'll talk to Israel and hear what he has to say."

Hector's eyes became wild.

"Hector, you'd better back off. Nicky is getting really mad," Albert warned.

But I could see that Hector was in need of a lesson. I spun and grabbed his shotgun.

"You want to challenge someone?" I snarled. "Challenge me. What do you want? Knives? Guns? Fists? You call the game and I'll play it anyway you want!"

Hector knew I was serious.

"OK, OK, OK, Nicky!" he muttered.

But the matter wasn't closed.

We all knew Wilkerson had to die. It was just a matter of how to do it without hurting Israel.

My intention was to see Israel alone the next day. But when I found him, who should be with him but Wilkerson.

"Hey, Nicky," Israel called, motioning for me to cross the street to where he and Dave stood talking. "How about going with me to a meeting tomorrow night, Nicky?"

"Naw, I don't wanna go," I said, staring my hatred at Wilkerson.

Israel insisted. "Nicky, you're a chicken. That's it! You're afraid to go."

"C'mon, Israel," I muttered. "Cut it out!"

"Nicky's a chicken! Nicky's a chicken!" Israel's sing-song cut deep into my pride. He cupped his hands around his mouth and began to call out to the whole neighborhood.

"Nicky's a chicken! Hey, Nicky's a chicken."

Everyone could hear.

I burned with embarrassment.

"Hey! Israel, you know better than that. You know I'm not chicken. You know I am not afraid of this guy or God or anybody. Leave me alone, Israel, OK?"

"Aw, come on Nicky, why won't you come?"

"I'm just not going to."

"Because you're chicken. You are afraid of God and this guy. It's the first time I've ever seen you afraid."

I glared at Israel.

He was possibly the only person in the world who could say such words to me. I glanced at Wilkerson, who was grinning innocently.

The man was dead already, I swore.

Wilkerson would not get away with this.

11

Pregnant By The Holy Spirit

I didn't know anything about the Holy Spirit that day on the street. Being born of the spirit meant nothing to me.

But a birth was about to happen.

Somewhere in this world a human infant is born every minute of the day. Until the moment of birth, babies exist peacefully in the security of the womb.

Some are born in anticipation and great joy. Others are utterly unwanted and even abandoned.

Once outside the safety of the mother's body, the baby clashes with the harsh reality of a cold, cruel world — pain, rejection, humiliation.

Who can predict at the moment of birth a child's future? That is a mystery locked in time. Only the passing of years will reveal whether the newborn will be a future president of the United States, a senator, a psychiatrist, a lawyer, a preacher, a rock singer, a scientist or a movie star. On the other hand, the baby also can grow up to be a Mussolini, a Hitler, a Lenin, a murderer, a drug addict, a prostitute, a homosexual, a traitor — or a disgrace.

Weeks before that night when I had gone to get Israel's OK for David Wilkerson's murder, the preacher and his wife, Gwen, had been preparing for the birth of their third child.

Time for delivery of the baby drew near as Dave busied himself with his little church in Phillipsburg, Pennsylvania. Then, as he was idly leafing through a copy of *Life* magazine one day, Dave's attention was sparked by a news story of teen violence in New York City.

Michael Farmer, a crippled man killed by a vicious gang, was featured in the article. As Dave read about the street gangs and the crime wave in the streets, he was shocked.

He poured over the details and photos.

"Go to New York, Dave," a voice whispered within.

"I'm just imagining things," he muttered to himself as he continued reading.

Again the voice spoke.

"Go to New York, Dave."

This time he began to pray and ask the Lord if the message could possibly be from Heaven.

"Yes," came the answer, "go to New York, Dave."

"Lord," Wilkerson cried, "how can I tell Gwen? You know she's about ready to have our baby."

After a long session of prayer, Wilkerson knew it was God's voice he had heard, so he rose to tell Gwen.

In spite of the unreasonable timing of God's call, Gwen fully realized that if the Holy Spirit was instructing Dave to go, he had to go.

The example of Jonah made that clear.

Wilkerson would have to go to the Ninevah of the streets.

No other choice remained.

By all human standards of reasonable conduct, going to New York City at any time for Dave Wilkerson was foolhardy. He was leaving a small country town for the largest city in the United States.

He had never been there before nor been exposed to the coldness and cruelty of the slums.

He knew nothing about reaching hardened street people. As if that were not enough, he had a family and a pastorate.

Going to New York made no earthly sense.

Any thinking person would have said, "Dave, you've missed the voice of God."

But Wilkerson listened only to the inner voice, laying aside his questioning.

He headed for New York.

If you've read *Run Baby Run* or *The Cross and the Switchblade* or seen the movie, you know the rest of this story.

Things didn't go well.

Trying to talk with the arrested gang members at the Michael Farmer trial, Wilkerson got into trouble with the judge and police.

Confused, he wandered into our neighborhood and the street corner where I first saw him. His preaching was so charged up with what he believed that it amazed me.

I thought he really had guts to stand there and talk so boldly about Jesus Christ. After he had finished preaching, someone pointed me out to him saying, "If you can reach Nicky, you can reach anyone." David Wilkerson walked up to me, looked me straight in the eyes and said, "Nicky, Jesus loves you." I couldn't believe what I heard.

My only defense was to start swearing at him. As I walked away, I hoped not a soul detected how threatened I felt in the presence of a man whose words and actions I couldn't fathom.

Wilkerson was undaunted as he followed me to the Mau Maus' basement headquarters. Again he spoke out, "Jesus loves you, Nicky!"

I spat at him, then I slapped him.

He didn't slap back, so I pushed him down. Then I cursed his God, his mother, Jesus and anyone I could think of that might mean something to him.

He pulled himself up from the floor where I had flattened him, looked me in the eye again with no evident malice and said, "Nicky, Jesus loves you."

Sleep wouldn't come that night. I kept hearing his voice saying over and over, "Jesus loves you, Nicky. Jesus loves you, Nicky ..."

The only place Dave could locate to sleep was in a nearby church. There, stinging from my humiliation of him, he waited for God to send him back to his family. He trembled with self-doubt, wondering if he had been mistaken about his mission — if he had embarrassed the Lord instead of lifting the Father up.

Almost ready to give up, he began to suspect that he had, after all, missed God's direction.

Even so, he remained in constant prayer for me. The burden of my soul never left him night or day. Yet it all seemed so hopeless. Everyone Dave talked to tried to discourage him. "Nicky's the worst. He'll never change. You're wasting your time."

But God had put an incredible love for me in Dave's heart.

Even though he was intimidated by the circumstances, he continued to pray — four hours daily. From 2 a.m. until 6 a.m., he poured out his pain and asked God to perform a miracle in my life.

A small turning point for me was a following day when Wilkerson gave his shoes to a guy named Jo Jo — who had none. I watched Wilkerson do it, and I knew there was something in that man that defied human explanation.

It scared me.

Anything even slightly related to the supernatural shook my confidence, so I shut out the meaning of his action. But I knew he was penetrating the Mau Maus gang as no one ever had before.

My best friend, Israel, began listening to Dave. Israel was telling the guys that things could be different, that they could really change.

While I consciously resisted what he was saying, on an unconscious level some deep yearning awakened.

A tiny wisp of wondering rose within me. Words did not accompany the feeling. Only a faint question mark hung within my heart.

Outwardly I continued to denounce him and verbally abuse him.

I continued to proclaim that I hated and despised the man's guts.

And I did.

But I was mystified by him, too.

I feared him.

I wanted him dead — and out of my life and out of Israel's life.

Well, as you might guess, especially if you've read the books or seen the movie, I didn't kill Wilkerson.

I brought the whole gang to his meeting — where we proceeded to whoop it up and try to disrupt everything.

Then, he asked for volunteers to take up the collection.

HA! I was on my feet in an instant, picking out five Mau Maus.

And Wilkerson trusted us.

He let us take up the offering.

When it was time to take it up to him, my friends were all grinning at me — knowing that now we would split with the loot.

But I couldn't.

Something important was happening.

A baby was being born.

As everyone gawked, I turned the money over to Wilkerson and returned to my seat.

During the altar call, I felt crushed by my sins — and conviction that Wilkerson's words were true. With Israel and the rest of the gang, I stepped forward. As Wilkerson prayed over me, he told God that I was very lonely.

I looked up, not understanding how Dave knew.

And I saw Wilkerson was weeping, his lips trembling. He was in the presence of Jesus Christ, his friend and savior.

I stared at this man, touched deep in my soul — not knowing Dave was spiritually in labor, feeling the pain and believing the "baby" would really come forth.

The Holy Spirit touched Dave's words as he prayed for me, "God, you placed Nicky in the womb of his mother and you love him."

Then, I, the "baby," began crying — crying in repentance. I was on my knees, torn apart and broken. I began to feel God's love and understand the tenderness of the one who brings life. My eyes swam with tears and my chest burned with a pain so intense that I could only call out the name of "Jesus!"

Throughout all his nights of intercessory prayer and all his days of pain, rejection and physical and verbal abuse, he had prepared for the arrival of a spiritual "baby." Now, Wilkerson delivered that baby and its name was Nicky Cruz.

It was as if I had gone back into the sanctity of my mother's womb. God flooded my heart with His divine love, peace, and security. More than that, he gave me a good friend who poured out his life into mine — painfully working to teach me and mold me over the next few years.

That night, I sensed for the first time in my life I was safe. Safe in the arms of Jesus.

A few hours later, Gwen Wilkerson gave birth to a baby boy named Gary. Today, Gary is a beautiful and tender young man who loves Jesus deeply.

Although Gary and I were conceived differently, we were delivered on the same day.

He was born for the first time.

I was born again.

12

What About The Others?

What happened to the rest of the gang?

Several of the several hundred guys and girls who called themselves Mau Maus gave their hearts to the Lord. Many fell away.

Albert didn't give his heart to the Lord, choosing instead to remain on the street. He was killed by police in a drug store hold-up.

Another, Marco, didn't come to the Lord, either. Long a dangerous, vicious, schitzophrenic street-fighter, Marco lost his mind shortly after his mother's suicide.

Willie died of an overdose and was found three days after his death in an old tenement building.

Hector is serving two consecutive life sentences in a Puerto Rico prison for murdering two men in a drug deal.

Quiet-but-vicious Carlos Reyes, one of the gang's strongest leaders, gave his heart to the Lord and is still faithful. He lives in Puerto Rico today.

What about Israel?

Shortly after Israel and I gave our hearts to Jesus, my new Christian friends decided that we needed to get out of Fort Greene until we were strong enough to resist our old temptations.

You see, in our neighborhood, a good kid really didn't have much of a chance without joining a gang. And in a gang, things were pretty evil — but different than if you were out on the street alone.

You could survive outside of a gang, but only if you were very strong.

So, it was arranged for Israel and me to go upstate. Somehow, something went wrong, though, the day that we were supposed to leave. I met our friends, but Israel wasn't there.

We left without him.

What we didn't know was that he had been waiting for us — and when he saw us drive away, he thought he had been betrayed, that our new Christian friends were purposely leaving without him.

He was furious. He threw his Bible away and cursed the Lord.

He went back to the gang and his old ways — convinced that the whole thing about Jesus was a farce, that our new Christian friends really didn't care anything about him.

Two months later, he and another gang member, Carl Cintron, were implicated in the killing of Tony Lamanchino, a member of a rival gang, the Angels.

Carl got life in prison — of which he served 16 years. Israel was sent to the penitentiary for five years.

Somehow, the Lord protected me from what was going on. When, out in California, I found out what had happened, I was heartbroken. But I couldn't do anything about it.

I wrote to Israel, but he didn't write back. So, I prayed for him. Fervently.

Every day —

Much like Wilkerson had prayed for me.

I knew Israel had enormous talent and potential that was going to waste. Israel was my best friend. He was closer to me than any of my brothers had ever been. I wanted him to really know Jesus' love — and see that it was real. I yearned for the assurance that I would be able to spend eternity in heaven with my friend, Israel.

Israel was different than most gang members — very intelligent, handsome and very trustworthy. He has a tremendous mind.

I wasn't able to go see him until he got out of prison. I came back from California and hunted for him until I found him in the Bronx one morning around 2 a.m.

We got things straightened out.

He forgave me.

And the Lord.

Today Israel is dedicated to the Lord and working as an evangelist in Washington state.

And Carl Cintron?

Recently he turned his life over to the Lord, too, at a revival in Brooklyn.

V

I Can't Seem to Forgive

13

Pedro

Where was I when Pedro was hurting?

Big, burly Pedro has disfiguring scars on his face. I put them there, back when I was a street punk.

As a result, Pedro had made a personal vow to kill me.

Somehow.

Someday.

Years after I became a Christian, he continued to stalk me. He hated me. He wanted me dead — evangelist or not.

He put me in the hospital with knife wounds — five days after my conversion.

The last time, he stalked me to a revival in Chicago. He showed up at the meeting with a revolver. The result was ... I guess I can only say it was "miraculous."

It's one more example of the devastating power of hatred.

And, conversely, the healing power of forgiveness.

Pedro's hatred toward me started back when I was a teenager. Pedro showed up in the Fort Greene slums of Brooklyn and started pushing kids and old folks around. He was strong and belligerant and he quickly developed a reputation of being a big bully.

He ran a floating dice game — and he made a lot of money because when he started losing, he would cheat.

Well, when he decided to move to my Mau Maus street gang's turf, we decided he had to be taught a lesson. We Mau Maus "ran" our neighborhood. We "protected" our merchants and residents. We were respected — in the sense that we were deeply feared and hated.

So, one day I pushed my way into his dice game and forced him to let me play. He didn't like it, particularly when I began to win in a big way. So, he stupidly tried to cheat me. I called him a punk and told him that although the little kids and old ladies thought he was a tough guy, he was nothing but a whimpering weakling — and that I was going to prove it right there.

Well, he pulled a gun and — to make a long story short — I pulled out my gun first and began hitting him in the face with it and with my fist, humiliating him in front of everybody. Finally I stuck my .22-caliber revolver's barrel in his mouth. Talking aloud I "tried to decide" whether or not to kill him.

I let him go — but I warned him to get off of our turf ... that the next time I wouldn't let him off so easily.

He backed off, but his pride was cut deeply. I had made him look very foolish.

He spat out a vow that I was a dead man.

I laughed.

But from then on, he had a deep grudge against me. He determined that he was going to see me dead. Well, I don't think it edifies anybody for me to tell all about the violent confrontations that followed. Once he and his friends almost killed me as they chased me through alleys and across rooftops.

It all amounts to this: Pedro and I were savages in an urban jungle.

One day, I heard he was up in a housing project with a bunch of people and his very beautiful girlfriend. So, I showed up and started making advances toward her — to humiliate him again ... and because I was somewhat attracted to her.

Pedro and I got into a very violent fistfight that ended with me kicking his own knife right into his face, then with me going crazy as I slammed his face into the sidewalk over and over, turning it into a bloody pulp.

As he writhed on the sidewalk, I began kissing his girlfriend and taunting him.

As he lay in the hospital, his determination to kill me became much more serious. Every time he glimpsed his permanently mangled face in the mirror, he vowed to see me dead.

I didn't care.

It's hard to explain my attitudes back then. But basically, I was a suicidal case. I was wild and drunk on death — and I didn't care whether I lived, as long as I and my friends were having an exciting time at the moment.

Then that all changed overnight when I turned my heart over to Jesus.

When Pedro heard that tough, crazy Nicky had turned goody-goody, he must have laughed. When he saw the stories in the newspaper about me and my friends and Wilkerson, he must have seen it as his chance.

His chance to even the score — forever.

He would jump me while my street-smart instincts were down — while I was off on this religious peace and love thing.

He began stalking me.

He didn't wait long to attack.

The first Sunday night after my conversion, he suddenly jumped me outside of church as I was walking down the sidewalk with a girlfriend of one of my newly converted ex-gang buddies. I'd really enjoyed the service. I'd brought 75 of my friends into the biggest service that little church had ever had. Sure, I was a little down since one of the ladies of the church had started lecturing me that I still had the long hair and jacket and jitterbugging walk of a street kid. But, still I was excited about Jesus and about how many of my friends had come to know him that night.

Well, suddenly Pedro came out of nowhere, slamming a knife into me without warning — his mind intent on my death.

Instinctively, I tried to shield myself with the only thing I had — my Bible. As Pedro jabbed the blade at my heart, he instead hit my Bible. I can honestly tell you that my Bible saved me physically that night.

But the next swing, he cut me — then he did it again and again, mostly on the hands as — unarmed — I tried to defend myself. As the girl shrieked and as blood went everywhere, I threw down my Bible and grabbed for an automobile antenna. Instinctively, I broke it off, intending to blind him, then go after him.

But then, reality hit me.

I was a new person.

And I understood why Pedro hated me. I sympathized completely. I had wronged him.

So, I began talking to the Lord out loud.

I dropped the antenna and exclaimed, "Lord God, I ask you to protect me. Help me, Jesus. I never expected to have to ask you something like this, but take care of me. I'm not going to fight this guy."

Pedro paused.

"What did you say?" he asked.

"I said that Jesus Christ is going to protect me," I answered.

Well, Pedro began cursing me and telling me that he was going to kill me right there and prove to everybody that I was never the tough guy that they always thought I was.

I knew he meant it.

"OK," I said. "Go ahead."

He stopped.

"Do you really believe all that?" he demanded.

"Yes, I do," I answered. "Jesus will protect me. I don't have to fight anybody anymore."

He stared at me — his hatred deep.

And then he walked away.

He could have killed me.

But he didn't.

As I staggered back to the church, the girl with me pleaded for help. I was rushed to the hospital where I had to undergo emergency surgery for the deep knife wounds on my right hand.

You can imagine that I had just a little confusion and turmoil as I lay in the hospital bed that night.

I felt as if I had been a coward.

I wondered if I had been a fool not to fight back ...

But ...

I could not deny that when I had called on the Lord to protect me, the attack had stopped.

After I had testified of my belief, Pedro had turned and actually fled into the darkness.

Then some friends came up to my room and told me that the Mau Maus had begun a bloody street war to avenge my attack and had beaten up several of Pedro's friends — and that he was in hiding.

So, there I was in the hospital, unable to do anything to stop it.

I was devastated. How could my friends, all of them new Christians, be doing this? How could they be acting like punks again, just to get somebody back for cutting me?

I couldn't believe it.

So, that night, alone in my room, I dropped to my knees and prayed, loudly, asking God to put a stop to all of this.

"God," I cried out, "I want you to help me. I don't understand any of this. God, I forgive Pedro. You know that I did far more to him that he ever did to me —"

And I just poured out my heart to the Lord.

I guess I had forgotten that I had a roommate.

He was an older man. The nurse had told him the complete story of my attack. Apparently he was really amazed with what he was hearing now.

"Young man," he called out to me in the darkness. "Do you believe that Jesus is that strong? And do you really forgive the kid that did this to you? Do you forgive the people who cut you up?"

I told him that I did.

In the darkness, he was suddenly down on his knees, too, crying. I didn't exactly understand what was going on.

"God," I prayed, not really knowing what to say, "I don't know what is happening. This man is crying. This man believes in forgiveness. I know you forgave me, now I ask you to forgive him."

That was when he really began to open up in his own way and asked Jesus into his life.

I didn't see Pedro again for several years. But I heard that he was still after me.

Yet, I was at peace.

I had forgiven him.

I had put myself into the Lord's protection.

So, Pedro could stalk me all he liked.

I belonged to Jesus.

I was at a crusade at a big auditorium in Chicago when I saw him next.

It had been five years since I had last confronted my old enemy.

I didn't spot him fingering his revolver up in the darkness of the second balcony.

I'd just been interviewed by the Chicago Tribune. The auditorium was packed with maybe 3,500 people. Another 2,700 had been put in an adjacent ballroom, listening over loudspeakers.

I preached about the simplicity of God's love and the healing that comes with forgiveness. I gave my testimony, telling how God can reach down into somebody who is 98 percent bad and make something wonderful out of the two percent good that is left.

I must have talked for about 20 minutes when I felt the anointing of God and began to go after the unsaved people in the crowd. That night it was as if I saw myself as a spiritual boxer, punching and jabbing my way into the hearts of the unbelievers — hitting them with strong conviction of the Holy Spirit.

It's hard to explain what happened during that message. I also was feeling their hurt and their pain and sorrow. And I knew their deep sinfulness and their their need for repentance and forgiveness.

I talked about how God had made me a new person.

I talked about Jesus' deep love and his open arms —

When I made the altar call, I broke down in tears and had to apologize. I said that I knew very strongly that there were people there that really needed this Jesus that I was talking about — and that I loved them.

Eight hundred and thirty people came forward.

I was leading them in a prayer for Jesus to come into their hearts and minds and spirits and bodies — and to take possession of their lives ...

Then I saw Pedro.

He looked more rugged than I had ever seen him before. His face was still marred from the times I had fought him.

His hair was long. He had a goatee. He was thin and hurting — and had been running from the law for a crime he had committed back home in New York City.

And now, this dangerous fugitive, this fleeing felon who had vowed repeatedly to kill me was pushing toward me, not praying. He was staring at me — deadly serious.

The people at the altar were crying with their faces down in tremendous personal remorse.

Not Pedro. He was pushing them out of his way.

"This is it, this is my time," I said to myself. "My date with death has finally come." It's strange to look back. I wasn't so worried about dying. I was worried that this was going to be a big embarrassment for the Lord, me being killed in the middle of this beautiful altar call.

"Oh, God," I prayed silently. "Let there be no sadness or sorrow here after we have had so much joy."

I began to walk toward Pedro, deciding that I would try to grab his hand.

"Nicky," he said, staring at me. "Nicky."

"Pedro," I answered solemnly, trying to see if he had a gun or maybe a knife.

"I want that Jesus," he said.

There were tears in his eyes.

"You've touched me," he was saying. "You've really touched my heart. I came here to kill you. I sat up there on the second balcony planning to blow you away. But you and these people have touched me.

"I want that Jesus.

"I want him now."

We embraced and I could feel the gun under his coat.

We knelt together, crying, hugging.

And he received Jesus into his heart.

14

I Can't Seem to Forgive

I will carry the memory of Pedro's forgiveness as long as I live. You would think after such an amazing instance of God at work, I would never again struggle against another human being.

If God could work such enormous forgiveness in me toward a man trying to kill me, surely everything would be downhill from then on.

Well, it wasn't.

Recently, I found myself wrestling internally with a "brother" in Christ.

Not winning, either.

By then, I knew what the Bible had to say about forgiveness.

I also knew how serious the consequences to those who refuse: physical illnesses, emotional problems, spiritual ineffectiveness, other Christians hurt and ministry weakened.

Futhermore, I knew it was the right thing to do.

So, what hindered my progress toward obeying God for almost two years?

Why couldn't I forgive my brother in the Lord?

Bitterness.

This brother had spent money my ministry had raised to reach the lost. He had spent it in ways which I would not have spent it.

We were of different minds. He did not share my vision. His heart was not one with mine. I did not see the necessity of many of his expenditures. He did not understand my frugal nature — and irritation at going into debt.

I wouldn't bother to unfold this episode in my life were it not for the certainty that I am far from being the only Christian or Christian leader ever troubled with such bitterness.

An unforgiving spirit is a crippling poison.

It will drain the life from churches and Christians and evangelistic outreaches.

For that reason alone it is worth every effort to communicate my story.

Just what is forgiveness?

Dictionary definitions won't do here. I knew them all.

I was wracked with agony.

For two years, I wrestled with bitterness and self-pity — so much that I began to lose my enthusiasm for the ministry. My family became concerned.

I couldn't leave behind my anger and sense of betrayal that somehow my ministry found itself $200,000 in debt.

From my darkening perspective, trusted Christians had tried to rip my ministry from me. As a result, I was struggling to keep things afloat financially. I had to dip into the royalties from my books to pay ministry expenses — which was especially difficult since I had set aside the royalties to pay my daughters' college tuition.

God's command that I ought to love my enemy didn't cool the angry flame burning within.

I had been betrayed, I felt.

As I assessed the full scope of my ministry's economic losses, I found myself withdrawing inwardly. Surely this went beyond ineptitude, I said to myself.

My mind wandered during conversations. I only pretended to listen.

Although wonderful friends reached out in unexpected ways, although Jesus was faithful, walking with me in my dark valley, I allowed my bitterness and unforgiveness to fester.

In the middle of my most earnest prayers, my mind would wander and I would see the face of the man I now considered my enemy — glaring down at me.

"God," I would cry, "how could he have done this? Why did you let it go on for so long?"

Of course, my prayers went unanswered. God does not bless our accusations against our brothers.

My efforts at pulling together the scattered pieces of my spiritual life were unfruitful.

After two years — why couldn't I forgive and forget?

Why couldn't I forgive and go on?

I was indulging in a huge "pity-party." I was so engrossed in trying to establish the rightness or wrongness of specific actions that I plunged myself deeper into the abyss of despair.

I felt my personality changing as I wrestled with my pain. God let me wallow around in that pit long enough to become so sick of it that I was willing to do anything rather than remain.

But I continued in ministry.

Even though I was sick at heart.

Hurting.

Bitter.

And increasingly discouraged.

After a speaking engagement in Atlanta, I boarded the plane mechanically with nothing on my mind but getting home.

Exhausted after my series of meetings, I let my mind coast into neutral — ignoring the torrential rainstorm.

The nightly preaching had worn me out — particularly in my bitter, angry, defeated, depressed state of mind.

As I fastened my seat belt, I leaned my head back and closed my eyes. Surely no one would be tempted to try to talk to me.

The plane sped down the runway and into the air.

Something inside me came to life. My eyes simply would not remain closed. But the severity of the storm outside my window only depressed me worse. The sullen gray of the skies tightened around my heart.

I longed for sunlight.

"How thick is this miserable cloud?" I wondered as I pressed my face against the window. My body, mind and will cried out against the blackness choking my life and my ministry.

Then the airliner broke through the clouds.

Suddenly my spirit soared as we entered a drastically different world. My eyes were almost blinded by the brightness of the sun shimmering off of billowy, white clouds.

The pure blueness of the sky leaped out at me. Every fiber of my being was shaken by the beauty of God's heavens. Tears streamed down my cheeks.

I was filled with supernatural joy. Peace I hadn't felt in months swept through me.

Suddenly, I was shaken back to reality as a flight attendant leaned forward and touched me on the arm.

"Is anything wrong?" she asked in concern. "Can I do something for you?"

"No, no thanks," I said with a sheepish grin. "Nothing."

She offered the complimentary glass of champagne that other attendants were handing out.

"No thanks," I said.

But still, I could see her consternation at seeing a man cry in public.

"I know you can't understand what is going on," I finally said. "It's just that for months I have been crawling around in a dark valley of despair — something like the darkness of those skies over Atlanta.

"When the plane pulled out of the clouds, I saw the dazzling light of God's real world. I can't explain it but something happened inside. I really don't understand what it was."

Still uncertain, she sent the captain back to make sure I was all right.

My joy at discovering he was a Christian merely intensified the experience. He understood. My heart was free for the first time in months.

And I saw my problem from God's perspective.

I had usurped his role.

I had attempted to be judge and jury.

Only God knew the heart of the man I had chosen to consider my enemy.

Judgment of my Christian brother rested entirely in his hands, not mine. I didn't know all the facts. I couldn't see inside my brother's heart.

I could not discern mistake and inexperience from dishonesty and corruption.

These months of trying to determine who was right and who was wrong had been beside the point.

What did that matter?

Glorifying God was the issue.

Preaching to the lost was my call — not attempting to convince God of the guilt of the one I felt had betrayed me.

God showed me that I was not responsible for the errors that had occurred. I was, however, deeply responsible for one thing, my continuing, poor reaction to the problem.

Never mind if I had a right, humanly speaking, to be bitter.

Did my reaction line up with the Word of God?

What was it Jesus said?

"Father, forgive them, for they know not what they do."

That was it.

If Jesus living inside of me could forgive those who murdered him, could he not do the same thing in me?

I know I couldn't do it for myself.

I had tried all this time.

But could he do it for me? Another Scripture came to mind: "... Forgiving one another even as God for Christ's sake has forgiven you."

Of what did God forgive me?

I thought back to the enormity of His forgiveness for all my rottenness.

How had I forgotten during these long months? I saw that to forgive is basically to give up my right to hurt someone who had hurt me.

That was it!

What a breakthrough after months and months in my long, dark tunnel. My mind cleared as sweet waves of forgiveness washed over me like the ocean. Energy returned.

Fresh insights into God's heart opened.

I sat down with my wife and began to see how she had been right — she had been telling me to take my eyes off of my defeats and instead look at my victories.

I realized what strength the Lord had given me when he blessed me with my family. I began once again praying with them and studying the Bible with them.

Yes, we are supposed to be one in Christ. Yet, in my martyr's mindset, I had been shutting out the little ones who loved me and who the Lord had given me to show his ways.

I saw that an unforgiving spirit doesn't remain safely in our mind or heart.

It spreads cancerously.

It had permeated the whole of my life — truly threatening my family and my ministry far, far worse than the original poor use of funds ever had.

I had become increasingly ineffective in every facet of my being as I dwelt on this growing, festering fury in my heart.

I had taken my eyes off of Jesus and attempted to take all my burdens onto my own shoulders.

I had been like a crippled person trying to run a marathon.

I had given Satan an entrance into my life — and when he gets his foot in the door, he always moves in to occupy, vandalize and confuse.

The foothold had become a stronghold.

And only by following Jesus' forgiving example could I expel him.

Only one action on my part would close the door and push him out again — wholehearted forgiveness. To forgive is to forget.

Forgiveness is a choice, not a feeling.

15

How Can You Forgive?

We must choose to forgive.

Are there consequences for not forgiving?

Mental anguish, depression and confusion are just the beginning. Thanks to God's intervening grace, I was spared the full gamut of what could have happened.

But I see those consequences operating in people wherever I travel.

On December 23, 1982, a young man home from college for Christmas break was hit head-on by a drunken driver. Ted Morris, 18, died four hours later.

Ted's parents, Frank and Elizabeth, were devastated. Hatred filled their hearts when they thought about a stupid drunk wiping out a life so filled with promise.

These parents were Christians, but they felt justified in their anger.

"Deep down I was terribly unhappy with myself," Elizabeth told me. "I knew I should forgive, but instead I hated. It was ruining my life. I gained weight, I lost interest in my appearance, and I withdrew from people. The more I hated this man who had needlessly killed my son, the more miserable I became."

Only a light sentence was imposed by the court — five years probation plus a jail term to be served on alternate weekends.

Frank and Elizabeth were enraged.

Then Elizabeth attended a meeting where Tom Pilage, the young man who had killed her son, was speaking on drunk driving and its tragic consequences. How well I knew them, thought Elizabeth.

When he made reference to the accident, Elizabeth was certain he would say it couldn't have been avoided. People get drunk all the time, you know.

Instead, he admitted that he was a murderer.

He told the audience how sorry he was, how guilty he felt, and that he knew he did not receive the punishment he deserved.

Elizabeth then went to visit him and invited him to her church.

"I forgive you," she said. "But you must forgive yourself as well."

Something broke inside of her, she told me. Suddenly, her mourning was over. Her bitterness was gone.

Tom began going to church with the Morrises and now has become a close friend.

Forgiveness healed Elizabeth Morris — and Tom Pilage.

Wherever I go, people constantly ask me to pray for healing, or prosperity in financial crisis, or against continual attacks of Satan in their lives. Instead of praying immediately, now I inquire whether they are harboring unforgiveness.

It is amazing what ugliness surfaces as I probe a bit.

To pray for them is useless if the root cause is an unforgiving spirit. Unforgiveness allows Satan an entrance into our lives and jeopardizes everything that we love — family relationships, careers, ministry, physical and mental health.

Forgiveness. There is wonderous healing through its release. It generates within us a joy and freedom we cannot possess normally. It may involve a supreme effort on our part, but it is always possible — and worthwhile. Forgiveness is giving up my right to hurt someone who has hurt me.

What happened when I gave up the bitterness I had harbored — the anger and unforgiveness that had almost destroyed me over that two-year period?

God in his miraculous way repaired our finances. He sent me solid friends who quietly contributed both large and small sums so that we could meet our obligations.

The Lord also sent me a new administrator — June Creswell. She had been saved through our ministry 13 years earlier. So, when she heard that we needed somebody with her particular skills, she was delighted to come on board and get things straightened out.

Today, we owe nothing to anybody.

Forgiveness.

It must be unconditional.

We are commanded to love our enemies — pure and simple.

Then God will be faithful to you in your hurts and needs.

He will provide healing.

Will he mete out justice?

Think about that. Do you really want the Lord to take vengence on you for the wrongs you, too, committed?

Of course not. So, don't pray that he take vengence on anybody else. To be truly just, God would also have to give you the punishment that you deserve for hurting others.

Be thankful for his forgiveness.

And forgive the ones who hurt you — and love them.

That means that if the man who I convicted in my heart for his management of my ministry's funds walks up to me, I must welcome him and embrace him and love him. After all, God forgave a young street hoodlum who robbed little old Jewish ladies, defaced rivals' faces and plotted to kill an obedient, naive Pennsylvania preacher.

God says, "If you do not forgive, your heavenly Father will not forgive you." That's pretty scary.

God didn't say it would be easy to forgive.

He only said it would be worth it.

When we are alone and hurting, we have a choice.

To sit in our self-pity and our anger and our bitterness — and refuse to forgive and go on with life.

Or we can step forth into joy.

Into peace.

Into healing and restoration.

Into ministry and fulfillment.

Into forgiveness.

VI

No Turning Back

16

A New Beginning

One night when we were holding a crusade in the war-torn Central American republic of Honduras, several members of my evangelism team were holding a street meeting.

In the middle of it all, a drunk came up to the front and started making a pest of himself.

My friend, Dr. Jerry Kerner, ignored him and tried to preach while several of the Christians tried to talk to the drunk and calm him down. However, he got louder and more obnoxious — and started cursing my friends.

Well, one of the new Christians, a Honduran girl suddenly had enough. She'd been reading her Bible and didn't see any reason that she couldn't invoke Jesus' name in the situation — just as the Apostles had and as the Bible says we should.

So, since she wasn't as theologically astute as the rest of us, she didn't know any better than to stand up, point her finger at him and declare with authority:

"In the name of the Lord Jesus Christ, I command you to shut up. Shut your mouth. In fact, I call on you to fall!"

Well, the drunk stared at her in surprise.

And then he fell flat.

You can explain that however you like. But he was out cold.

And here's the real miracle:

A few minutes later when he sat up, he was stone sober. He looked up, dazed, as the believers knelt around him. Somebody asked if there was anything they could do for him.

"Well," he said cautiously, "I'd really like something to eat."

And just like in the story of the little boy with the fish and loaves, there was an Indian lady in the crowd who had come into town with a big bunch of bananas on her head.

Bear in mind that she had come in to sell those bananas — they were her livelihood.

But the Lord had so touched her that she pushed forward and offered her bananas to the now-sober drunk.

Both of them turned their lives over to Jesus that night, there on the street of Tegucigalpa, the capital of Honduras.

A simple story.

But Dr. Kerner told me later how the simple incident had touched his life.

"I am not the same," he said afterward.

Well, ours is a simple gospel.

When I was a new Christian, I lived in a simple world, too. Dave Wilkerson and a handful of Bible school teachers were my only models for a long period. Perhaps it was natural for me to suppose that all Christians were great men of God like them and operated with a similar degree of fervor and commitment.

Disillusionment awaited such a naive perspective. When church people and staffs of Christian organizations did not measure up to my preconceived notions, I was plunged into bitter disappointment. Too immature to realize that I would always be disappointed if my focus remained on people, I spent much time groveling in the pit of perplexity.

Climbing out was a long process.

But growing up in Christ always is. Even though consistency and total commitment ought to be the earmark of the church and its constituency, the truth is (whether we like it or not) it's not always there. Of all people, shouldn't Christians understand the importance of commitment and how to accomplish it?

But we are too content to leave the job to somebody else — even if we are perfectly equipped for the job.

I've been guilty of that, too.

Once, right after I had come to know the Lord, I was living at the Teen Challenge center and a man called me and asked if I would pray for his daughter.

"Sure," I said. I was pleased to pray for anybody — particularly for them to come to know Jesus.

"Thank you," the man said. "My daughter is crippled and we believe that she can be healed."

I gulped.

Healed? This guy wanted me to pray over a crippled girl? And he was expecting that she would walk as a result?

I tried to keep my composure. But I knew I had to get out of this one. I wasn't any faith healer. I didn't have "healing hands." My ministry was evangelism — and it still is.

I hungered and thirsted after getting people saved.

But healed?

"Look," I told him, "I don't want you to lose your faith or be discouraged if nothing happened. I'm really not the one who needs to pray for your daughter."

But the guy insisted.

And he said that he would be bringing his little girl to a church where I was supposed to be the guest speaker that night.

Well, I was in a fix.

When I arrived at the church, I was pretty nervous. But it got worse when I looked out over the congregation. There was the guy, waving at me from the back to let me know that he was there.

With his crippled little girl. And more than 25 relatives.

As you can imagine, I was extremely uncomfortable throughout the entire service. I kept crossing and uncrossing and recrossing my legs and trying to decide what I was going to do.

Then as I closed my sermon, the man came up with his little girl.

I took a big gulp.

The whole family had arrived — and apparently all their neighbors and distant relatives, too.

"Here," I said to the church's pastor. "I think you should handle this."

"Oh, no," he refused. He didn't want to pray for her, either. If she wasn't healed, it would make him look bad. That might cause him to lose his pastorate. But if I looked bad ... well, I was leaving anyway at the end of the service, he probably figured.

So, I laid hands on the child like I had seen other people do. I prayed, asking the Lord to heal her.

What happened next was nothing but spectacular. As I prayed and as the family prayed and the congregation prayed and the pastor prayed, I could hear snapping and popping.

I could feel the little girl's bones and tendons straightening out.

Miraculously.

Before my eyes, the little girl's legs took the proper form. She stood and walked for the first time in her life.

She was healed.

How?

It certainly wasn't because of my faith. It wasn't because of any miraculous touch from me, either.

But because of her healing, that night 22 members of that family fell to their knees and accepted Jesus.

I have looked back in years since and understood how it was my place to pray for that child as the family lifted up their great prayers of faith.

Could I have kept the miracle from happening?

I think so.

I could have shrugged off my duty.

The miracle might have gone undone.

I believe this may explain why churches and parachurch organizations are experiencing so many problems.

We are called.

But we do not answer the voice of the Lord. We pretend that we do not hear his urging.

We make excuses and say that it's not our job.

Perhaps that is the most crucial problem churches face today. We have developed a false faith — a faith without commitment.

We are busy running around to Bible conferences and retreats, searching out the most eloquent expositors of the Bible, and racing to weekly Bible studies to fill our heads with more outlines and formulas. Meanwhile, millions of hurting people all over the world are dying without hope.

We are called to reach out to them.

Individually, we each hear from the Lord.

But we're too busy to respond.

It might take a commitment involving more time than we are willing to give.

Commitment.

What is commitment all about?

Commitment simply means to devote ourselves unconditionally to the Lord and his work. We stick with the job before us, despite circumstances.

It means teaching a Sunday school class every Sunday — no matter what — and allowing the kids in that class to become the most important youngsters in the world to us. It means interceding for them and taking time during the week to find out what is bothering them.

Commitment does not take into account convenience, or the changing whims of emotion.

True commitment remains an enduring thing — that which can be counted upon. Marriage is a good example. Not too many years ago, divorce was virtually unknown. Even if a marriage deteriorated behind closed doors, dissolving the contract was unthinkable.

This is not a discussion of the pros and cons of staying in a bad marriage. It is merely to observe that just two short generations ago people honored their commitments even when faulty.

"A man's word is his bond" once ruled business transactions.

You didn't need contracts or intricate legal documents to make sure a person kept his promises.

Today, the fear of being "taken" begets a mistrust of everyone. Consequently, it forces us to read between the lines, search the hidden messages, and take every precaution to outwit the other before he outwits us.

No wonder stress-induced, degenerative diseases ruthlessly strike down more than half of our adult population with alarming regularity.

Look at motherhood, for another example. In the "old days" mothers were committed to their children come hell or high water. It mattered little if the children proved deserving. A mother's devotion remained undying and could be compared almost to God's.

What a contrast to the picture today. Women still bear children, but if they are not disposed of before birth, they often become an unwanted commodity forced to shift for themselves while mothers pursue their own lives.

Children are placed in professional child care centers before they can speak intelligently. Prior to that, a baby-sitter is hired so that mom can rush back to work within the prescribed two-week maternity leave.

Where did we lose it?

Asking that question is like trying to determine the onset of cancer. Some authorities state that by the time a victim discovers a malignancy, he probably has had it more than 39 months. That's a frightening realization to contemplate:

To determine the precise beginning of the decline of integrity in our nation is equally impossible.

This creeping malignancy was spawned in a variety of sources, among them the infancy of the humanism barely flourishing a century ago.

The truth is, this degeneration happened so quietly, so subtly, so slowly, that suddenly we woke up one day to find that we no longer lived in a Christian nation.

The full-blown disease had spread to every spot of our society.

We couldn't believe it. It was inconceivable that while we dozed, God had been tossed out of the public schools and nativity scenes had been banned from city halls.

While America rotted from the inside out, most of us were happily climbing the ladder of prosperity and materialism. Too late we woke up to the awful truth that somehow the Lord's work had been ignored while we scurried to pay for two cars and a nice house with a pool.

Naturally, we expected other professing Christians and Christian organizations to be doing the job while we couldn't.

And so now, we blame the "clergy" for falling down on the job. I'd like you to find that word in the Bible. Instead you will find that we are all called to ministry and commitment.

The trouble is that either we won't, or we don't know how to do it. Most Christians don't even know how to be fully committed to the Lord.

Let's get down to the bottom line.

I, personally, believe the reason the members of the body of Christ are not committed is that we are too caught up in our own lifestyle.

We live from Monday to Saturday in any fashion that satisfies our changing whims. On Sunday we get together to romance each other and report how wonderful it is to be a Christian. Pastors are afraid to teach discipleship because they might offend someone and lose out in the "numbers game."

As a result, church members today want to be entertained — not committed.

And we run the risk of being like the church at Laodicea, mentioned in the Book of Revelation — we're lukewarm, wishy-washy, do-nothing Christians due to be spewed from the Lord's mouth — and sent forth into outer darkness.

I say that it's time that pastors quit trying to relive the Book of Numbers and concentrate on experiencing the Book of Acts. That's not just a clever phrase — I mean that it's time that we quit counting bodies and began requiring *ACTION* of those sleepy people in the pews.

Look at what happened to Communism in the 1900s. Lenin introduced communism, and by 1917 took control of Russia with only 40,000 followers. Today communism controls over one-third of the world's population. Why? Because people committed themselves totally as individuals and in groups to a common cause. Lenin said, "Give me a handful of dedicated people, and I will take the world." One of today's young communists said, "We communists have a high casualty rate. We are the ones that get shot, hung, ridiculed, fired from our jobs, and made as uncomfortable as possible. We live in virtual poverty. We keep track to the penny of every cent we make, and we spend only what is absolutely necessary to keep us alive.

"We have been described as fanatics. We are fanatic. Our lives are dominated by one great overwhelming factor — the struggle of world communism. It is my life, it is my people, my religion, my habit, my sweetheart, my wife, my mistress, my bread, and my meat. I work for it in the daytime, I dream of it at night. I cannot carry out a friendship, a love affair, or even a conversation without relating to the force that both guides and drives my life.

"I have already been jailed because of my convictions, and, if necessary, I am ready to go before a firing squad."

As Christians, can we claim such an in-depth commitment?

"God intends for us to prosper," I hear people saying.

Or, "I'm a child of the King. What's wrong with having everything I want? Christians are crazy to go around with a poverty complex."

Maybe that's true. Now that God was blessing my ministry with an unusual amount of success, I was forced to consider these questions. Is it true that because God's Word teaches we are children of a King, we should lack nothing of this world's supply?

Naturally, such teaching holds a tremendous attraction.

Who wants to be poor?

Who wants to do without when others seem to have it all? It's no wonder this theology has gained such a foothold in the church today.

But is it scriptural? Is it even practical in the working out of Biblical principles in our lives?

Would I dare step off into this appealing doctrine and expect God to prosper me because I am faithfully serving Him? These and other considerations became issues I needed to face early in my ministry.

One of the most humorous columns ever printed was written by Bill Willoughby, the Religion News Editor of the *Washington Star* in the nation's capital. He did a story on Rev. Ike, a preacher in New York City who proclaimed the "Gospel of Good Fortune" from his pulpit in a very flamboyant way.

This preacher could see no merit in being down on one's luck, Willoughby pointed out.

Rev. Ike proposed that the real Good news is that people no longer have to be poor. "The lack of money," he said, "is the root of all evil" (a slight perversion of the actual Biblical statement: "The love of money is the root of all evil.")

Well, let me tell you that both statements are true. I grew up as a poor kid, and I've worked much of my life among extremely poor people. I know more than I want to know. The lack of money for many people is the root of all sorts of evil, and they do some pretty strange things — things they might not do if they had a little more money.

On the other side of the coin, however, there are those who never have enough money no matter how much passes through their hands.

For both groups, money constitutes the root of evil, but not in the Scriptural sense.

Rev. Ike usually preached to people who never had enough money. He set a literal example for them.

He was chauffeured to church in the flashiest and most expensive automobiles available, and even though his suits were garish, he paid inordinately high prices just to display the image he was trying to communicate.

His strategy involved working up the crowds into a kind of tempo and convincing them that if they would give their money to him they could expect God to multiply it many times over.

Hundreds did exactly that.

They put their money at his disposal, and there were clear-cut results.

Richness came — for Rev. Ike.

Even though I don't agree with Rev. Ike, I respect him for this reason: He is upfront with his intentions and motivations.

Rev. Ike tells his followers, "If you believe money is the root of all evil, then give your money to me."

What I don't like are those who use their "Christian" vocabulary to manipulate believers.

Jesus never had a checking account or an American Express Card and he never used his name to promote himself or gain wealth, yet his name is being used to make billions of dollars.

I have heard evangelists brag about holding only two or three meetings a year. Why travel more when they can depend on their mailing list for two or three million dollars of financial support each year? This is a sad, pitiful, devastating statement of their lives.

Their first love was to go out and place the hand of a lost and dying world in the hand of Jesus.

Now, they are content to remain in one community and teach those who already know the Lord. I feel such an evangelist has backslidden from his calling and lost his first love.

His commitment has shifted from people to money.

Because of my uniquely different background — born in the underdeveloped country of Puerto Rico as the eighth child in a family of 18 children, my formative memories consist of life with only bare necessities.

The children of America would consider my childhood home with its total absence of necessary facilities as immensely deprived.

And it was.

But finally things changed.

Now I could choose.

Would I use my early deprivation as reason to make up for what I lacked then? In my mind, I knew I could easily rationalize to the point of appearing spiritual.

God is so good.

He is making up to me for what I missed during childhood.

Or, I could go to the opposite extreme and assume that to be truly spiritual, one must be poor as well.

Having lived so many years in a state of poverty, probably I was more comfortable that way because it was the known.

The unknown can be frightening.

For these reasons and conflicting theologies regarding money and the Christian, I have often been confused in my thinking. The problems stemming from my past created inhibitions, and I've always felt the necessity of being over-cautious as to the salary I make, and the impression I am making — especially since my life is so open, so lived in the public eye.

I don't mind the pressures of living that kind of life.

I simply want to do my best for Jesus and be a strong witness for Him.

Fishbowl living does present special problems though.

Traveling as extensively as I do, I find that people are always wanting to give things to me.

For a long while I couldn't seem to handle this graciously because I honestly felt undeserving of such gifts — especially from people who have so little that anything they gave me was a sacrifice.

Often I found myself rejecting these gifts for the simple reason that I was too embarrassed. "Just send it to Nicky Cruz Outreach," I would mutter as I brushed them aside.

Then one day a friend sat down with me. "Nicky," he said, "as your friend I need to talk to you about a matter that's bothering me deeply."

"Sure," I agreed, "whatever it is, tell me."

"Do you realize, Nicky, that you often offend people? Well-meaning people who only want to thank you for sharing Christ with them."

"What are you talking about?" I asked. "I'm talking about people who give you gifts. You act as if you don't even appreciate them. You just give them away to someone else because you feel guilty receiving them."

I knew he was right. I had been wrestling with the problem for a long while, and I never seemed able to resolve it.

"What will people think of me?" I wondered. "Will they suppose I'm trying to take advantage?"

"Nicky, I understand the problem you are having, but you can't stop people from wanting to give. That's just a natural expresssion of the love of God in their hearts. It is a way for them to thank God for the blessing you have been to them. Don't you see how important it is for you to be a gracious receiver as well as a giver?"

This was something I had to deal with myself.

Frankly, I was devastated at my friend's rebuke because I had such a desire to do the right thing, to respect motivations for giving and not to exploit people.

How could I think of committed widows and elderly giving their last checks and know that they were taking food from their mouths to help support my ministry?

I agonized over the question of whether we were using that money conscientiously enough to reach people for Jesus Christ.

The Apostle Paul had problems, too. He apparently experienced similar wrestlings. He wrote that he "worked night and day, laboring and toiling so that we would not be a burden to any of you" (2 Thessalonians 3:8).

He spoke of the suffering he endured for the sake of the Gospel, and that suffering was a part of his ministry here on earth. Giving of himself was more important than taking from the people he served.

On the other side of this picture is the promised blessing to those who give.

"Give, and it shall be given to you, good measure, pressed down, and shaken together shall men give to your bosom"

Whatever I did, it was not for me to rob people of this blessing because I couldn't bring myself to receive. The most important thing to me then, and now, continues to be what God's Word teaches on any subject. Apart from that consideration, I knew I had no ground to stand on.

Without even studying, I thought about the men and women who make up the drama of the Bible.

Were most of them materially prosperous? I could count only a few, and those few came from wealthy families. Many of them lost their wealth or gave it up, like Barnabas, for the work of the Lord.

The most notable New Testament characters I could remember came from what we would call "blue-collar" occupations; fishermen, carpenters, skilled and unskilled laborers. The Apostle Paul may have been wealthy to some degree, but I recall that he said, "What

things were gain to me, I count them but loss
... and have suffered the loss of all things."

Where would we be today without the
invaluable "prison epistles"? If Paul had
questioned God's goodness in allowing him to
suffer such indignity and deprivation, we
wouldn't have them.

Didn't he insist that his being in prison
turned out to be a divine bonus? "What has
happened to me has served to advance the
Gospel," he said.

Oh, that each of us could have the fervor for
evangelism that filled Paul. Singlehandedly —
at the direction of the Holy Spirit, he spread
Christianity across the Roman Empire.

He didn't want wealth.

He didn't care if he lived or died.

Hebrews 11, the great faith chapter, speaks
of those who "wandered about in sheepskins
and goatskins, being destitute, afflicted and
tormented."

They are among the "heroes of faith" listed
in God's annals.

Committed.

Dedicated.

To God and his people.

17

No Turning Back

Have you ever stood before a sea of people and asked God to stop a thunderstorm — and watched it pause until the sermon was over?

I have.

Have you ever been shot at by an unknown assailant while preaching to an enormous crowd? And not known that an associate had been wounded *by the bullet intended for you* until you had left the crusade site in a station wagon being carried on the shoulders of 20 enthusiastic believers?

Those two incidents happened two days apart on two different continents.

As I look at what they represent, I stand in awe at what God has done with a dead-end dropout who could barely speak English.

And I stand humbled that God allowed me to have the desire of my heart — after I obeyed him.

Twenty-four years ago as a new Christian in Bible college, I determined that God would be first in my life. We had a beautiful father-son relationship.

My heart's desire was to minister in a Spanish-speaking country. I thought God could use me in Latin America because of my culture and background.

Imagine my surprise when the Lord said, "No, I want you to remain here in the United States. This is where I found you, saved you, cleaned you up, and filled you with my Spirit."

While I understood total commitment, I also knew I had a choice.

I could obey. Or I could *insist* on doing things my own way.

But did I want to wander around the wilderness for 40 years like God's ancient Israelites? Remember: they could have made the trip from Egypt to the Promised Land in 11 days instead of those 40 years.

Thus, I decided to follow God instead of Nicky Cruz — in obedience.

In commitment.

God once asked Solomon what special gift he would like — power or riches or fame ...

Or ...

Or whatever Solomon's heart desired.

Solomon chose wisdom.

The Lord was so pleased with Solomon's commitment that he gave him all the other things as well.

That's what happened with me.

I obeyed the Lord and accepted a ministry in the United States — despite my poor English, my heavy accent ... and my burden for Latin America.

At first, Gloria and I were truly happy to graduate from Bible college and go to work for Teen Challenge back in Brooklyn — working with addicts and problem kids and gang members.

Our weekly salary was $12, but we weren't caught up in the business of living, only living for Jesus.

And Jesus blessed us.

A purity of love for others characterized our life then. We were truly committed!

As time passed, I must admit that I lost some of my "spiritual virginity." Books had been written about my life, movies were made — then I wrote my own book. I became well-known and lived a comfortable life.

Then God revealed to me through difficult circumstances what a victim of selfishness I had become.

I realized that I had a choice again — just as we all do. Once more, either I could continue doing things "my way" (which I dearly loved), or I could return to doing it God's way.

God's way is the only way.

The Bible is full of true-life warnings — lessons from history that illustrate what happens when we choose our own way instead of the Lord's.

Every Biblical character who successfully served God possessed a unique brand of unswerving allegiance to the Lord's cause. But they were ordinary people just like you and me.

They became extraordinary only by this single quality:

Commitment.

Take Joseph, for instance. When you read the exciting drama of his life, you sense that he was an obnoxious little kid, committed to the Lord, but who severely irritated his ten older brothers.

After he humiliated them one time too many in front of their father with his self-righteous visions from God, they decided to rid themselves of his holy little presence.

At first they were going to leave him in a dry well to die. Then, cooler heads prevailed and they sold him as a slave to a passing caravan.

True brotherly love, wouldn't you say? Joseph must have been an unprecedented little pest.

Here Joseph's story should have ended — except ...

Except that this committed little boy didn't waver in his trust and dedication to the Lord. So God blessed him. Joseph thrived in what should have been hellish circumstances.

Without the Lord's protection, he might have disappeared into the ranks of expendable laborers in a desert copper mine or as human chattel manning the oars on an Egyptian galley.

Instead, he surfaced as the slave of a powerful Egyptian official named Potiphar. Quickly Joseph rose through the ranks to become chief overseer of all of Potiphar's possessions. So trustworthy was the young Hebrew that Potiphar soon put him in charge of his day-to-day operations.

Then Potiphar's wife found herself drawn to Joseph. There can be no mistaking her intent. The New International Version of the Bible translates her proposition quite bluntly: "Come to bed with me!"

What normal, red-blooded man could resist such a temptation? Her husband would never find out. He was far too busy. And he trusted Joseph completely.

The key to Joseph's refusal is wrapped up in his reply to her: "How can I do such a wicked thing and sin against God?"

Against God.

Joseph's commitment was far deeper than to his earthly master.

And the Lord raised him up to be second in power only to Pharoah — the king.

Because of commitment, Joseph could stand strong when assailed by the winds of temptation.

Commitment.

It is not born and bred into a human heart. It is an acquired, learned behavior — and it usually begins in early childhood. The problem is that most of us today missed this training in today's permissive environment.

So if childhood is the only time when we can learn to be committed — some of us are doomed

But it is not. And we are not.

My own experience provides ample proof.

If there was anything I did not receive while growing up, it was parental instruction in commitment.

I was the eighth of nineteen children born into a home where Satanic spiritualism and superstition prevailed.

If my integrity depended upon childhood training, there would be no hope for me.

But regardless of heredity or lack of it —

Or our early training ... or lack of it —

No matter how devoid of integrity our lives have been —

There is hope.

It comes through a new beginning.

A new beginning with God.

What was it that the Lord required of me?

That my ministry was to be in the United States — and not in Latin America.

When I obeyed — concentrating my energies here, the Lord began dropping little tidbits in my lap.

Invitations to Latin America came in — not to open up a ministry or to undertake long speaking tours or to set up an evangelistic organization in South America.

Just invitations.

To visit.

To speak.

Then the invitations opened up worldwide.

It was in Caracas, Venezuela, South America that I was speaking to 20,000 people gathered on an open athletic field. At least 4,500 made public decisions to follow Jesus.

Then, during the altar call, somebody took a shot at me.

Apparently at the very moment that the shot was fired, I stooped over. The bullet whizzed past — striking one of the native pastors on the platform. He didn't really know anything had happened until he looked down and was perplexed to find that his shirt was covered with blood.

Not wanting to disrupt the service, he slipped away to a hospital without telling me he was hurt.

How could such a terrible thing happen?

I don't know.

But the Lord protected us. The pastor recovered fully.

After the service — although none of us knew about the shooting — my friends began to fear for my safety — particularly when the crowds began to press in around our station wagon, wanting autographs, wanting to shake hands or tell us about their lives.

So 20 young men picked up our car and carried it safely out of the crowd.

That was a rare experience.

The next day, I was in Johannesburg, South Africa. There, over several days, I spoke to enormous crowds — including 22,000 people who gathered in a growing thunderstorm the first evening.

At first I was going to try to speak under an umbrella.

Then, I decided that if all those people could get wet just to hear me, then it wouldn't hurt me either.

But it was cold, so, I looked up toward heaven, and asked the Lord to stop the rain.

And he did.

That made the national newspapers.

Jesus plainly said, "I am the way, the truth, and the life. No one comes to the Father except by me."

Thus, you can see my commitment to him.

If Jesus spoke the truth, then he is our ticket. Only by surrendering our will to him by faith can we receive power. Only through him can we turn things around and make our lives worthwhile.

Perhaps you don't have this power because you do not have a Savior or a Lord.

No amount of resolve or human effort can make you a Joseph.

That only happens in humble surrender.

Instead, the heart of Judas Iscariot is within us all. The Bible tells us that every human being is "deceitful and desperately wicked."

Only the indwelling presence of Jesus Christ replaces the stuff of which we were originally made.

When we commit our lives to him, the Lord himself becomes our source.

Raising us up in the midst of our enemies.

Giving us the desire of our hearts.

Prospering us in Egypt.

Protecting us from gunfire in Venezuela.

Stopping thunderstorms in South Africa.

18

Where Is The Balance?

Travel into underprivileged countries constitutes a large part of my ministry — primarily because most of the countries in the world are economically depressed.

What I see is enough to wrench my heart from its moorings.

While American Christians sit in front of their televisions listening to the latest version of the Greed Gospel, millions in the Third World own little more than the clothing they wear.

As Americans gather into their "bless me clubs" — bowing to the false god of money, most of the world lives in hovels without even the bare necessities of life.

I was miserably poor as a child.

Yet by comparison, my Puerto Rican family was unspeakably better off than many to whom I preach.

As I view such poverty, I think of the greed back home in America and the popular prosperity message.

How many of these religious celebrities are supported by naive Christians who believe the money is going to missions?

We read of some television evangelists living in extreme luxury, their lifestyle one of extravagance.

Yet, they beg and cry on the air for money — while millions starve.

All I can determine from reading God's Word is that this is not the spirit of giving he intends for his children.

It is a spirit of greed.

A worship of money.

I cannot condone it, and I will not allow my wife or my family to participate.

God has provided sufficiently for our needs.

What is left over should go to spreading the Gospel in this world.

One of the reasons I find it so difficult to see conscientious believers sacrificing to give generously to such ministries is because there are many such evangelists who abuse their status.

Their promises are manipulative — promising to pray personally for viewers needs, when in fact they never see anything but a sampling of the prayer requests.

Keypunch operators answer the letters with staff-written, computerized responses especially designed to convince the viewer that the evangelist has written them a personal letter.

In fact, these beloved "partners" are merely a number in a data bank.

It is true that ministries need money to accomplish what God has called us to do.

But I personally cannot endorse the techniques and false promises behind the new "greed gospel" — the "God-wants-you-rich" theology.

I fear for young ministers taking up such a mantle — looking at God as a way to make money.

That kind of incentive is going to cause an evangelist to fail miserably — spiritually, ethically and morally — although not necessarily financially.

Perhaps I am stepping on too many toes.

I fear that I am even offending some of my dear friends in the ministry.

Yet, I have to ask a tough question:

Can we in America enjoy luxurious lifestyles while 80 percent of the people in the world go to bed hungry every night?

Thousands starve to death every day.

How can we continue to justify our extravagance, our waste, and our clamor for more, more, more?

Where Is The Balance?   181

Certainly America has been blessed.

I do believe we are reaping from the heritage of our godly ancestors. Most of them were people of integrity, adhering to strong Christian faith and convictions, ascribing to stern work ethics and thriftiness.

They earned for us a prosperity beyond imagination.

There are many godly people today who are wealthy, striving to be good stewards of God's plenty.

Their examples inspire the rest of us, and without them the spread of the Gospel of Jesus Christ would be greatly curtailed. Who could be critical of such faithful followers of the Lord? That, however, is not the issue.

Are we to believe their pattern is the one we should claim and aspire to?

Where is the balance?

We are only told to give happily to the Lord. In his time and in his way, he will return it.

God promised to "supply all your needs according to His riches in glory by Christ Jesus."

Promises of sufficiency for His children abound throughout the Bible.

The solution for me is to focus my eyes on Jesus, trust his promises for the supply of my needs, and go about the business my Father called me to do.

VII

Just Lift Up Your Eyes

19

Gizella

Where was I when Gizella was hurting?

Gizella was a junkie. A heroin addict without hope.

Without God.

Without forgiveness.

She wasn't the sort of addict that you and I normally think of. She was a pretty Hungarian girl on the streets of Budapest, behind the Soviet Union's Iron Curtain.

My heart aches for Hungary. Once a dominant power in Europe, Hungary was defeated in World War I and stripped of her empire.

In World War II, Hungary sided with the Nazis and, in Hitler's defeat, was invaded by the Russians.

The Soviets have never left. A puppet Communist government was forced upon the Hungarians in the late 1940s.

Yet, Hungary retains many ties to the West.

And like the West, Hungary has terrible problems today. The first time that I visited Hungary's capital, Budapest, I immediately sensed the oppression there. It went far beyond the tight security at the airport or the 136,000 highly visible Soviet Bloc troops in the streets.

Perhaps you remember the 1956 uprising in which Hungary's prime minister, Imre Nagy, declared his nation neutral and appealed to the West to throw the Russians out. The Allies did little, however.

The Soviets crushed the rebellion with tanks. They installed Janos Kádár as premier.

Today the Soviets treat Hungary just a little differently than the other countries of the Eastern Bloc. Things are easier in Hungary. There are more consumer goods.

Yet, morale is poor. The family unit is breaking down. There is rampant cynicism and despair. Suicide is a major problem.

Nationwide, there is serious alcoholism and drug abuse — even among adults and professional people. Among the youth, there is an epidemic of heroin addiction.

Gizella was one such addict. I met her at an anti-drug abuse conference in Budapest. Incredibly, I was the principal speaker, invited by the Hungarian government — which is officially Communist and God-hating.

Somehow, the Lord had put *Run Baby Run* into various atheist officials' hands and they had contacted me, asking me to come to Budapest to help them fight their drug problem.

You might ask: "How could you help the Communists?" Indeed, how can a Christian evangelist help a godless, Soviet-backed government fight drugs?

Flabbergasted, I asked myself the same thing.

And I asked, "Why me, Lord?" Why would they invite me? I am an American — the enemy. I think maybe my dark skin, my Puerto Rican accent and my Hispanic heritage somehow made up for that. The Hungarians looked at me as a member of an oppressed minority — a brother.

Well, I can only say, "Praise God!" that he prepared me in a way that they could accept me.

So, if I were to go to Hungary, what was I going to tell them when they wanted to know how to get their kids to get off of drugs?

They're atheists.

Maybe I could be arrested if I talked about Jesus.

Maybe I would be deported.

I didn't know.

But as I wrestled with what to tell them, I came to one answer.

I would tell the government officials about the healing power of Jesus' forgiveness — and how it was the answer to their drug problem.

If they asked me how I kicked drugs, I would tell the Communist officials about how Jesus had transformed me from a dead-end loser to the man they had invited to come give them answers.

If they asked me how I had helped others kick drugs, I would tell them about Jesus.

If they wanted to know about the programs that I had helped set up to help conquer teen drug problems or family drug problems — I would give them infinite details of everything they wanted to know.

But in order to tell them exactly what had happened, in every case I would have to tell them about Jesus.

You see, without Jesus, you don't get free of drugs.

So, the Hungarians sent for an expert in fighting their national drug problem.

And that's what they got.

But they also got an ambassador for Jesus.

Looking back, I can only marvel at what the Lord made happen.

As one of the conditions of my coming to Hungary, I got the Communist government to agree to print up and distribute 12,000 copies of my book *Run Baby Run* in Hungarian. As a condition of my next visit, they have agreed to print up and distribute 35,000 Bibles.

That's incredible, isn't it?

For 30 years, Christians such as Brother Andrew with his Open Doors organization have smuggled Bibles and Christian books behind the Iron Curtain, a few hundred at a time — at great personal risk.

I imagine that the copies of *Run Baby Run* that fell into Hungarian officials hands had been smuggled in by Open Doors — or one of the other groups answering the call to bring God's word behind the barbed wire of Eastern Europe.

And now, with a single motion of God's hand, the atheist Hungarian government is printing up and handing out Christian books and Bibles.

How can all this happen?

Easy. God loves Hungary.

Think about it. If the Lord can love a murderous thug in the streets of Brooklyn, then he can certainly love Communists, can't he?

Well, in the few days that I was in Hungary, the Lord allowed me to spend time with the precious, bold brethren of the persecuted church there.

They, too, don't have it as bad as elsewhere in Eastern Europe. Kádár has been quoted as saying that he doesn't care if a Hungarian citizen goes to church on his own time — or to a soccer match for that matter; that it is the citizen's own business. Also, parents are permitted to teach their children about the Lord.

But don't mistake me.

These people are persecuted. Yet in the midst of it, they love the Lord — and they love one another.

The first night that I was in Budapest, the hall was packed with perhaps 3,500 government officials, medical workers, social specialists and others engaged in the anti-drug fight. There was an amazing excitement, too.

I talked about suicide and drugs and the family. I talked about how the Bible says a family should be structured.

And I talked about how Jesus wants us to live.

Did the officials cut me off?

No!

It was amazing!

They listened carefully to everything I had to say. I talked on and on and on for about two and a half hours in the first session.

I could have spoken as long as I wanted.

The power of the Lord was there.

Then, I offered an altar call.

I just felt the Lord's peace to offer a chance for the government officials to accept Jesus.

Were we all arrested?

No.

More than 1,100 people gave their hearts to the Lord — doctors, psychiatrists, nurses, therapists, social workers, government officials and Communist party members from all over Eastern Europe.

It was unbelievable.

All of these were employees of Soviet-backed governments. This was a government function.

We could all have been thrown in jail.

Yet, they calmly put their lives and their careers on the line as they publicly accepted Jesus.

They didn't do it quietly, either. Eastern Europeans are emotional and expressive.

The second day, we put on a banquet for the Hungarian government officials who had invited me — and for all the pastors that we could reach.

And it was wonderful.

It was powerful.

I felt like Jonah in Ninevah. A supposedly wicked government was falling on its face in repentance before Almighty God.

It was the most exciting thing I have ever seen.

The Lord gave my interpreter a powerful anointing. He preached — not just translated. He was smart — sharp.

He was under the power of the Lord. And he got through to these tough government representatives and medical officials, many even from outside of Hungary.

There were some very tough questions. Sometimes they tried hard to trick me and trip me up. Several times, I just had to tell them I didn't know the answers to their questions when it got down to specific medical and psychological terminology.

But when I told them what I had seen working in drug rehabilitation, they listened. Why? Because I was telling them the only answer that was going to work for them —

Jesus.

I told them about Teen Challenge in Brooklyn — about how it was a kind of Holy Ghost hospital, where the Lord put people back together.

I told them the only force behind any successful program had to be Jesus.

And right there, people attending the conference began giving testimonies — of how the Lord already was restoring their families, returning their children to them, delivering them from drugs and alcohol, and giving them true love and hope.

Eagerly, the officials listened and accepted what we had to say.

It was incredible.

It was as if we all had stumbled out of a vast desert and the Lord had prepared an enormous fountain. We all drank and drank and drank of his goodness and his salvation and his healing. And we were refreshed.

It is hard to describe.

But let me tell you, Hungarian Communist officials were coming to the Lord that afternoon.

Will it make a difference?

What do you think?

Today in Hungary, 10 Christian books have official government approval. That may not seem like much right now. After all, in America every week, at least 10 new Christian books are released.

In Hungary, the Communist government will permit its citizens to read only 10 — total.

But at least there are 10.

We have to start somewhere.

Today as I write this, the most popular one is *Run Baby Run,* particularly among Hungary's youth.

And that takes me back to Gizella.

She had gotten hold of a smuggled copy of *Run Baby Run* through the underground — long before I got there. She had read it and she wanted to know if the answers I offered in it were real for her.

I first saw her in the afternoon of the second day that I was in Budapest. She was tiny and obviously sick from drug use.

As I was coming into the conference center, she and some people with her came toward me.

"Are you Nicky Cruz?" she asked me in a thin, weak voice. "Are you the real Nicky Cruz?"

"Yes," I responded, surprised.

"Look," she told me through my interpreter. "I have read your book and this is my last chance — this God, your God that you talk about in your book. I'm a drug addict. I just got my friends to bring me here straight from the hospital. I wanted to see you before —" I could see the terrible turmoil in her beautiful, blue eyes. "I'm dying inside," she rasped. "This is my last mile. What can you tell me?"

There was death in her voice from years of drug abuse.

"I want you to know that the same Jesus who changed me can change you," I told her. "I don't want to get sharp with you, but you can understand this one thing: He died for you. For you he came. You are precious to him. He loves you. Everything he touches he changes. He can touch you and change you right now."

Then I said a little prayer.

As I prayed, she put her head on my shoulder — she was that weak.

And I said, "Tonight, I want you to come to my meeting. I don't want you to take any more drugs or anything."

"I haven't taken anything today," she said. "I wanted to be sure of what I was doing."

"I want you to come tonight," I told her.

Gizella

She promised me that she would be there.

And then she left me and I went up to my room.

Let me tell you, I was exhausted. The Hungarian officials and brothers seemed to want every minute of my time that they could get.

That night, we held an impromtu meeting in a Catholic church. The priest was attending the anti-drug seminar, had read *Run Baby Run* and felt that the Lord wanted us to have a chance to speak to the people.

I don't know how he got word out about the meeting, but the church was packed when I arrived. It could hold about 2,500 people, but more than that were packed outside and someone set up closed-circuit television so that people could watch from the parking lot and all the other rooms and the foyers.

I don't want you to think that they were all Christians.

Not by any means. The priest hadn't gotten the word out to his faithful little-old-lady, Altar Guild members. He had sent tips to Communist party high-ups, the police, Army officers, medical officials and workers in the Communist bureaucracy.

As word spread, we also attracted a lot of curiosity seekers.

State-run television channels sent over camera crews. The national TV network sent a

Communist propaganda-trained interviewer. On camera I talked with them about Jesus. And he listened, respectfully, and asked good questions.

He asked my wife what she thought of Hungary and Gloria answered that she thought it was beautiful and that the people were beautiful — which he seemed pleased to hear. I think maybe he expected Americans to be critical and rude.

Then, he came back to me and asked about the miracle of Jesus Christ healing drug addicts — and wanted to know how such a thing could happen.

So, right there on Communist-run television, I told him. I told him all about it. And he let me talk at length.

He asked me what I came to Hungary to do. I answered that it was simple — I hadn't come to criticize or to try to change Hungary, but to bring the beauty that Jesus Christ could give.

I said that I didn't have the power or the education to bring all of Hungary to Jesus, but I could bring Jesus to Hungary.

He seemed very impressed.

Let me tell you, the whole thing was a miracle.

The Lord was with us. I didn't talk politics — I talked Jesus. Every 30 seconds — Jesus — so they couldn't edit it out when he got back.

Then, the camera crew set up to broadcast our meeting.

On Hungarian national television.

I spoke for 45 minutes and they recorded every bit of it.

Right in the middle, I was passed a note. It was about Gizella.

I had seen her in the auditorium and she was obviously in serious pain from complications of her drug withdrawal. She was sitting with her friends and a nurse from the hospital.

The note said we had an emergency, that Gizella wasn't going to make it.

She was dying.

They were going to take her back to the hospital.

So, right there, in front of the television cameras, I asked believers to stand, that we were going to pray together that the Lord would touch her, save her and heal her as a testimony that God is a God of power.

I didn't realize it, but the television crew knew her. Apparently, Gizella was very well known.

They knew that she wasn't faking.

So, I prayed that God would raise her as a testimony that he is still working today with the same power that he had 2,000 years ago. And all the believers in the auditorium began praying — and I mean loudly.

Then, I thanked God for the healing as five government doctors in the crowd — three women and two men — got up and helped take Gizella out.

I continued with my testimony.

As I came to the end, there was a noise backstage behind me.

It was Gizella.

She stepped out, changed — newly strong. With her were the five state-paid, Communist doctors, exclaiming about what had happened — that she had been healed right before their eyes.

Boldly, they proclaimed their belief that Jesus was real and that he alone was the answer to Hungary's drug problems.

Then, for two minutes, Gizella talked into the microphones, telling of her miracle.

The believers in the crowd erupted in joy and praise and celebration as the TV crew took it all in, and as other doctors and people who knew her wept — accepting Jesus, too.

My joy was overflowing.

I thought my heart was going to burst with happiness.

For across Hungary unbelievers saw and believed.

From the Catholic Church's sanctuary and the foyers and the parking lot, 1,300 people crowded to the front and to the altar to accept Jesus for the very first time — while the

Christians in the crowd prayed and praised and sang out their unspeakable joy.

It was as if an angel had come with a trumpet and announced to Hungary's shepherds that the baby Jesus was born. As I stood there, the Lord touched me, as if to say that this was the one day for which he had prepared me all of my life.

He had taken me, a simple dropout from the streets of Brooklyn — now 45 years old — and he had brought me here to confound the wise of Communist Hungary — and to show them irrefutably that Jesus truly is alive.

And standing there, I experienced the wonderful peace of knowing I was flowing in God's will, that I had been allowed to be a part of his great plan.

The people began singing.

"Do you realize how much these people love you?" I asked Gizella. "Did you realize they all were praying that the Lord would heal you and raise you up."

"Yes!" she exclaimed into the microphones, her voice strong and excited. "Yes!"

"Is there anything you want to tell them?" I asked.

"You know me," she proclaimed to the crowd. "My veins are clean. My mind is clear. I am restored. Jesus is Lord! I heard the voice of Jesus tell me, 'You are my daughter and I love you.' "

And then she began to speak to the parents of drug addicts — telling them not to give up of hope, that suddenly she had been filled with a great love for her mother and father.

"I'm going to go back to them and let them know that Jesus is Lord and that he is real. I got him today and I'm going to keep him always."

It was hard to leave Hungary.

I had been there only two days.

But the Lord had transformed a mundane conference on drug abuse into a nationwide revival — with the tacit approval of an ordinarily godless government.

As my family and I sat on our plane, we were filled with joy — and with a heaviness. We didn't want to leave.

We had been changed.

We loved Jesus as never before.

We'd had an incredible glimpse of his power and his majesty.

God is not frustrated by atheistic bureaucrats.

What has happened in Hungary since our visit? They've allowed two drug rehabilitation centers to open — teaching and preaching the undiluted and healing power of God's forgiveness. A third is preparing to open.

I've been invited back.

And God is continuing to move in Hungary.

There's a revival underway there that nobody will be able to stop. Because of years of persecution, the believers there don't fight and bicker with each other. They aren't worked up over who is Catholic or who is Baptist or who is Pentecostal.

Instead, they work together because they love Jesus.

As a result, his healing and forgiveness are sweeping over a country that you and I would consider to be nothing but an atheistic wasteland, an enemy.

Like Ninevah in Jonah's day.

A wicked nation.

Falling to its knees.

Repenting.

And receiving healing.

20

Just Lift Up Your Eyes

Where was I when Hungary was hurting? Where were you?

Is it possible that you and I are too wrapped up in our own hurts and loneliness to be touched — or to care about a bunch of Communists thousands of miles from our cozy, comfortable homes?

In Matthew 9:13, Jesus spoke to the Pharisees, "I have not come to call the righteous, but sinners."

That's why I went to Hungary.

That's why I'm preparing to go to the Soviet Union and Poland. And to Central and South America — war-torn El Salvador specifically.

And to the violent streets of Miami.

And Philadelphia.

And New York City.

How can I do anything else?

Why do I leave Gloria and my daughters at home? Why don't I leave the work to somebody else? Why don't I stay home and send a monthly check to some nice missionary?

I heard God's call.

I read it in his Word.

I had to obey.

To whom should **you** preach?

The Lord will guide you.

Today in America it is illegal to take God's message into the public schools ... unless, of course, you are a kid.

That's right, if you are a Christian youngster, America's freedom of speech still permits you to talk about the Lord as much as you want in the public schools.

But you're the only ones now who can get in.

Young missionaries —

Wake up!

America's high schools need you. You are the only ones permitted to take Jesus inside.

And that goes for junior high schools, too.

And, of course, elementaries.

Third graders can win their buddies to Jesus. You bet.

Third graders can win teachers and principals to Christ, too.

Sixth graders can, too.

And kindergarteners.

He wants people to hear his message.

We just have to be willing to take it wherever he leads.

I am honored to take it — although there are times I can barely believe where I am being sent.

If I have the opportunity to preach to 10,000 people — and I suspect that it's a religious crowd in which maybe only 100 don't know the Lord, to whom do I preach?

I go straight for the unsaved — the 100 — and forget the 9,900. Why?

Because the final words of Jesus before he ascended into the clouds were plain: "Go unto all the world and preach the Gospel."

Too long we've been caught up by a spirit of religious apathy, lulled by an easy Christianity preoccupied with reconvincing those of whom are already convinced.

Too long we have dozed in our pews.

Yet, our own inner cities — filled with crime and horror — are ripe for harvest.

So are the suburbs!

And the little towns across America.

But where are the workers?

Remember the old hymn that goes:

"My house is full ... but my fields are empty. Who will go and work for me today? It seems like all my children want to stay around my table, but no one wants to work in my fields."

That's right.

Here in America, we have a glorious time fellowshiping with each other at Wednesday night potlucks, class parties, staff-deacon socials and whatever holy-looking excuse we can contrive to get together.

We sit around the Father's table, laughing and rejoicing. We feast in his blessings, claiming his material prosperity. We eat and play and laugh and sing church songs. We buy Christian rock records. We applaud TV evangelists.

And we hide in the temple.

Ineffective.

Silent.

Disobeying Jesus' Great Commission.

What about the millions who know nothing of our Father or our Savior?

They are not laughing.

While we are gathered together in our delightful little religious "bless me clubs," they are wondering why they should live another day.

Why is the spiritual harvesting equipment moving so slowly across the world?

. I'll tell you why:

Because we sit at home and wait for somebody else to go to Ninevah — while Ninevah is all around us.

Christians seem capable of thinking only of the question "Where were you when I was hurting?" Well, what about the hurts of others?

That's not somebody else's problem.

If you are seeking a real blessing, get involved. Take Jesus to your neighbors, to your buddies, to your co-workers.

The Holy Spirit will guide you, give you boldness and provide you with the right words if you seek him.

You will be filled with great excitement when you see yourself making a difference, when you see your friends changing from unhappy, unfulfilled pagans to joy-filled believers.

Go.

You may be the only person on earth who can speak to your best friend.

Dave Wilkerson may very well have been the only person who could ever have gotten through to me.

And I was quite possibly the only one who could win my friend Israel back into the Kingdom.

Look around you.

The church today struggles under the accusation God directed toward Ephesus. "I hold this against you: You have forsaken your first love."

What is our first love? The ministry of Jesus, Himself, is our best example. All of his energies were directed toward people.

People.

Your neighbors.

People.

The only eternally enduring entities in this world are people and the Word of God.

Not shrines.

Not Christian hotels.

Not temples.

Jesus focused on people.

Hurting people.

God's Word is clear:

"You say, 'I am rich; I have acquired wealth and do not need a thing.' But you do not realize that you are wretched, pitiful, poor, blind and naked."

When buildings, programs, ideas, innovations, symposiums, courses, seminars and conferences take precedence over the simple act of getting people to turn to Christ, we have lost our first love.

So, go!

Reach the lost.

Even if they're sitting in a church pew.

Even if they're in a Communist-sponsored anti-drug conference in Hungary.

Spread the word.

Do whatever it takes.

21

How Can I Obey God's Call?

What if you don't feel adequate in preaching to the lost — or witnessing to your friends who don't know Jesus?

I, too, doubted my call.

I read the Great Commission and just assumed that it was directed at somebody else.

I never dreamed God would call me to an evangelistic ministry when I went off to Bible college — straight out of the Brooklyn slum.

To say the least, I felt inadequate.

No, not just inadequate.

I felt the very idea that I could be a preacher was ridiculous.

Oh, I was willing.

But I was a street thug, a dropout, a former criminal who spoke terrible English.

Billy Graham I was not. I didn't even know proper table manners. In public, I was an embarrassment to my new Christian friends.

Robert Schuller I was not. Even today, I am not particularly eloquent — except as the Lord empowers me. I only speak from my heart as the Spirit of the Lord gives me utterance.

I'm not David Wilkerson. I owe everything that I am to Jesus, but without Dave's obedience to the Lord, and Dave's incredible patience and love for me, today I would be a forgotten street kid killed in the 1960s in some unnamed Brooklyn alley.

So, what am I doing preaching?

I was an unlikely candidate to enter an evangelistic ministry. But God gave me a burden.

He gave me a commandment. He gave it to you, too. Look in your Bible:

"Go ye therefore, and teach all nations, baptizing them in the name of the Father, and of the Son, and of the Holy Ghost; teaching them to observe all things whatsoever I have commanded you: and lo, I am with you alway, even unto the end of the world" (Matthew 28: 19-20).

But how could I preach? Moses, if you remember, complained that he couldn't talk. So, the Lord gave him Aaron to speak for him. Guess who the Lord gave me? Nobody.

I had no choice but to depend on the Lord to give me eloquence. In terms of natural talents, I was not born equipped for evangelism. Supernaturally, God had to give me the ability.

When I first felt God's call on my life, I resisted. Much like you are probably resisting right now. I protested.

Much like you are protesting silently right now.

I made long lists of excuses before the Lord — excellent reasons why I wasn't the one that he needed to go into the ministry.

I'm sure you've got similar lists.

To make matters worse, I really didn't have the vaguest notion of His direction.

How was I supposed to go into the evangelistic ministry? Where was I supposed to go? How? Where?

I had no idea.

And because of my swaggering, jitterbugging, arrogant ways, I really didn't get much encouragement from the Bible college faculty or fellow students. They couldn't believe that I was wrestling with Jesus' Great Commission.

They couldn't believe I would ever amount to anything. They figured I might end up as a church janitor.

I certainly didn't look like an evangelist.

Because of my thick Puerto Rican accent and my Hispanic heritage, I was judged as somehow different and unworthy for a large American ministry.

Well, I am a classic example of why your excuses are not good enough.

I am an example of God taking the weak things of the world to confound the mighty. In my meetings across the world, I attract thousands of adults, young people and teenagers — a large percentage of them non-Christians.

How? I am nobody.

Then, why do they come?

Because God has miraculously and supernaturally used Dave Wilkerson's book *The Cross and the Switchblade*, the movie — and my own *Run Baby Run* to get me into places where ordinarily nobody would want to hear me.

The Lord has done unbelievable things to get the books and movie into the hands of unbelievers — and has opened doors that ordinarily would have been nailed shut.

How else would Hungarian Communists get — and *read* — my book?

Our Lord wants the world to know the answer to loneliness and hurt: Jesus Christ.

Recently, he sent me to Spain — where it is next to impossible for a man of God to to get his message onto the television networks. Spanish television is closed to American evangelists. But somehow the Lord got me an invitation to talk on the evening news about my life. I was supposed to get three minutes.

Instead, they let me talk for 20 minutes.

Twenty minutes.

Can you imagine that?

Twenty minutes on Spain's evening news — me talking about how Jesus changed my life and how he is the answer to Spain's drug and alcohol problems.

When I got off the air, I started getting phone calls from the other Spanish networks. They wanted me, too, now. Would I come talk on their shows?

Incredible!

When I went to the Dominican Republic, a very poor nation that shares the Caribbean island of Hispanola with Haiti, I was invited to come talk to the president of the country.

How did he know about me?

The Lord had gotten a copy of my book in to him. He was very interested in hearing more.

During our crusade in Honduras, a reception was held and guess who showed up? All the rich people in the little country — the big landowners and jet-setters who control the Honduran economy. Why were they there? The Lord had circulated my book among them and they were very interested in hearing my testimony firsthand.

God is not limited by anything.

It is nothing but a miracle that after two decades the Lord continues to use my testimony to catch the interest of the unsaved in such diverse countries as Honduras, Hungary, Spain, South Africa and Mexico — and to pull them by the tens of thousands into soccer stadiums, coliseums and cathedrals to hear the guy David Wilkerson won to the Lord.

How does God do such a miracle?

Because he is God.

Once after I had told my story once again in the enormous Melodyland Church in Anaheim, California, my pride was hurting. "Lord," I prayed, "how is it that you have given me only one message? Am I supposed to tell my life story over and over for the rest of my life?"

The Lord's perfect calm came over me. "Nicky," his voice spoke into my heart, "continue to tell your testimony. I'll give you a fresh anointing every time."

I fell to my knees in humility, weeping.

I wasn't destined to be a theologian. "People can argue theology with you and win," the Lord said.

I was not to study to be a psychologist. "They can debate psychology with you and win," the Lord said.

Instead, I was just supposed to be a simple evangelist with one story to tell. "They cannot take your testimony away," the Lord said. "The Apostle Paul told his testimony over and over. So must you."

Today the Lord has been generous. In a crusade, he gives me messages that don't require me to tell my testimony over and over each night.

But it's the testimony that people come to hear. And it remains my most powerful tool to win the lost to Jesus.

So, you can see how I am living proof that God can use anybody.

Even you.

He can choose an unworthy person like me, bestow his grace on me — and open great doors of ministry.

He can and will do it to you, too.

How? Simply seek him and obey him.

Don't hesitate.

Obey.

With all the churches and professing Christians in the world, why are so few people, comparatively speaking, being won to Christ? Because we seem to believe that the job belongs to someone else — even while millions worldwide have never heard the name of Jesus.

Ralph D. Winters, a respected authority on world missions, tells me that:

• 27,000 ethnic groups live on our globe today;

• Only 10,000 of those have been touched by the Gospel.

• That leaves 17,000 or so ethnic groups without a church, a Gospel preacher or a single piece of the Bible or Christian literature in their language.

So, what are you supposed to do about it?

Go!

Where? How about next door to your hurting neighbor?

Wherever did you get the idea that the task is done — and that Jesus' return is imminent since we've done such a fine job?

No!

Go!

We've got a lot of work ahead of us.

Don't fall for Satan's deception that all is well. Don't be coddled into believing that we are doing good enough. We're sitting down in the middle of the last battle. We're dozing off while the enemy ransacks our homes.

Can you get off the hook by putting money in the offering basket?

No. Don't believe that you can buy off your obligation to the Great Commission.

Give, but also:

Go!

Speak Jesus' name!

Perhaps raising this challenge offends you. Perhaps you feel that I am some sort of radical. Perhaps you feel that your personal hurts and loneliness are far more important than the eternal damnation of your next door neighbor — or of millions in India or the Soviet Union or Uganda.

Well, I must speak my heart.

And I say that the Lord is telling you this very moment:

GO!

"You shall receive power," Jesus said, "... and you will be my witnesses ... to the ends of the earth."

Go!

Recently in Peru, I preached in a stadium that was so packed that people had to stand outside. When the altar call was made each night, people streamed forward. Over four nights, more than 17,000 people received Christ as their Savior.

One of them stands out in my memory.

A young lady was determined to climb onto the stage. Guards tried to stop her, but she would not give up.

"Let her come," I told them.

She poured out to me the details of a sordid life. She was a prostitute, drug addict and was tormented by lesbianism. God had so moved in her heart that she was determined to be free.

She was set free that night. Today, she is preaching the word.

My point? If God can use her ...

If he can use me ... then, frankly, you have no excuse, do you?

Let him use you.

Experience his joy.

Postscript

If you would like to know more about Nicky Cruz's work or would like to be a part of his ministry, write to him at:

Nicky Cruz
Nicky Cruz Outreach
P.O. Box 25070
Colorado Springs, CO 80936

MORE GOOD BOOKS FROM HUNTINGTON HOUSE

Inside the New Age Nightmare *by Randall Baer*
Now, for the first time, one of the most powerful and influential leaders of the New Age movement has come out to expose the deceptions of the organization he once led. New Age magazines and articles have for many years hailed Randall Baer as their most "radically original" and "Advanced" thinker ... "light years ahead of others" says leading New Age magazine *East-West Journal*. His best-selling books on quartz crystals, self-transformation, and planetary ascension have won world-wide acclaim and been extolled by New Agers from all walks of life.

Hear, from A New Age insider, the secret plans they have spawned to take over our public, private, and political institutions. Have these plans already been implemented in your church, business, or organization? Discover the seduction of the Demonic forces at work — turned from darkness to light, Randall Baer reveals the methods of the New Age movement as no one else can. Find out what you can do to stop the New Age movement from destroying our way of life. *ISBN 0-910311-58-7 $7.95*

The Devil's Web *by Pat Pulling with Kathy Cawthon*
This explosive exposé presents the first comprehensive guide to childhood and adolescent occult involvement. Written by a nationally recognized occult crime expert, the author explains how the violent occult underworld operates and how they stalk and recruit our children, teenagers and young adults for their evil purposes.

The author leaves no stone unturned in her investigation and absolves no one of the responsibility of protecting our children. She dispels myths and raises new questions examining the very real possibility of the existence of major occult networks which may include members of law enforcement, government officials and other powerful individuals.
ISBN 0-910311-59-5 $ 8.95 Trade paper
ISBN 0-910311-63-3 $16.95 Hardcover

From Rock to Rock *by Eric Barger*
Over three years in the making, the pages of this book represent thousands of hours of detailed research as well as over twenty-six years of personal experience and study.

The author presents a detailed exposé on: many current Rock entertainers, Rock concerts, videos, lyrics and occult symbols used within the industry. He also presents a rating system for over 1,500 past and present Rock groups and artists.
ISBN 0-910311-61-7 $7.95

The Deadly Deception: Freemasonry Exposed By One Of Its Top Leaders *by Tom McKenney*
Presents a frank look at Freemasonry and its origin. Learn of the "secrets" and "deceptions" that are practiced daily around the world. Find out why Masonry teaches that it is the true religion, that all other religions are but corrupted and perverted forms of Masonry.
ISBN 0-910311-54-4 $7.95

Lord! Why Is My Child a Rebel? *by Jacob Aranza*
This book offers an analysis of the root causes of teenage rebellion and offers practical solutions for disoriented parents. Aranza focuses on the turbulent teenage years, and how to survive those years — both you and the child!

Must reading for parents — especially for those with strong-willed children. This book will help you avoid the traps in which many parents are caught and put you on the road to recovery with your rebel.
ISBN 0-910311-62-5 $6.95

Seduction of the Innocent Revisited *by John Fulce*
You honestly can't judge a book by its cover — especially a comic book! Comic books of yesteryear bring to mind cute cartoon characters, super-heroes battling the forces of evil or a sleuth tracking down the bad guy clue-by-clue. But that was a long, long time ago. Today's comic books aren't innocent at all! Author John Fulce asserts the "super-heroes" are constantly found in the nude engaging in promiscuity, and satanic symbols are abundant throughout the pages. Fulce says most parents aren't aware of the contents of today's comic books — of what their children are absorbing from these seemingly innocent forms of entertainment. As a comic book collector for many years, Fulce opened his own comic book store in 1980, only to sell the business a few short years later due to the

steady influx of morally unacceptable material. What's happening in the comic book industry? Fulce outlines the moral, biblical, and legal aspects, and proves his assertions with page after page of illustrations. We need to pay attention to what our children are reading, Fulce claims. Comic books are not as innocent as they used to be.
ISBN 0-910311-66-8 $8.95

New World Order: The Ancient Plan of Secret Societies *by William Still*
Secret societies such as Freemasons have been alive since before the advent of Christ, yet most of us don't realize what they are or the impact they've had on many historical events. For example, did you know secret societies played a direct role in the French Revolutions of the 18th and 19th centuries and the Russian Revolution of the 20th century? Author William Still brings into focus the actual manipulative work of the societies, and the "Great Plan" they follow, much to the ignorance of many of those who are blindly led into the society's organizations. Their ultimate goal is simple: world dictatorship and unification of all mankind into a world confederation. Most Masons are good, decent men who join for fellowship but they are deceived, pulled away from their religious heritage. Only those who reach the highest level of the Masons know its true intentions. Masons and Marxists alike follow the same master. Ultimately it is a struggle between two foes — the forces of religion versus the forces of anti-religion. Still asserts that although the final battle is near-at-hand, the average person has the power to thwart the efforts of secret societies. Startling and daring, this is the first successful attempt by an author to unveil the designs of secret societies from the beginning, up to the present and into the future; and to educate the community on how to recognize the signals and to take the necessary steps to impede their progress.
ISBN 0-910311-64-1 $7.95

Hidden Dangers of the Rainbow *by Constance Cumbey*
The first to uncover and expose the New Age Movement, this national #1 bestseller paved the way for all other books on the subject. It has become a literary giant in its category. This book provides a vivid expose' of the New Age Movement, which the author contends is dedicated to wiping out Christianity and establishing a one world order. This movement, a vast network of occult and pagan organizations, meets the test of prophecy concerning the Antichrist.
ISBN 0-910311-03-X $7.95

To Grow By Readers *by Janet Friend / Marie Le Doux*
Today quality of education is a major concern; consequently more and more parents have turned to home schooling to teach their children how to read. The *To Grow By Readers* by Janet Friend and Marie Le Doux can greatly enhance your home schooling reading program. The set of readers consists of 18 storybook readers plus 2 activity books. The *To Grow By Readers* have been designed to be used in conjunction with Marie Le Doux's PLAY 'N TALK phonics program but will work well with other orderly phonics programs. These are the first phonics readers that subtly but positively instill scriptural, behavioral and moral values. They're a joy to use with the phonics program because no prior instructional experience is necessary. The *To Grow By Readers* allow parents and children to work together learning each sound. As your child progresses through the readers, something new is added, allowing your child to appreciate his or her own ability to understand and think logically about word and sentence construction, thereby raising the self-esteem and confidence of the child. You can lead your child step-by-step into the exciting and fun world of reading and learning, without heavy reliance on memorization. Repetition and rearrangement will leave your child begging to read page after page. Whether it's a home educational program or a phonics based program in school, these readers can substantially improve a child's reading capabilities and his/her desire to learn.
ISBN 0-910311-69-2 $64.95 per set

The Delicate Balance *by John Zajac*
Did you know that the Apostle John and George Washington had revealed to them many of the same end-time events? It's true!

Accomplished scientist, inventor, and speaker John Zajac asserts that science and religion are not opposed. He uses science to demonstrate the newly understood relevance of the Book of Revelation. Read about the catastrophic forces at work today that the ancient prophets and others foretold. You'll wonder at George Washington's description of an angelic being which appeared to him and showed him end-time events that were to come — the accuracy of Nostradamus (who converted to Christianity) and the warnings of St. John that are revealed in the Book of Revelation — earthquakes, floods, terrorism — what does it all mean? No other author has examined these topics from Zajac's unique perspective or presented such a reasonable and concise picture of the whole.
ISBN 0-910311-57-9 $7.95

Backward Masking Unmasked *by Jacob Aranza*
Rock music affects millions of young people and adults with lyrics exalting drugs, Satan, violence and immorality. But there is even a more sinister threat: hidden messages that exalt the Prince of Darkness!
ISBN 0-910311-04-8 $6.95
On cassette tape! Hear authentic demonic backward masking from rock music.
ISBN 0-910311-23-4 $6.95

Personalities in Power: The Making of Great Leaders *by Florence Littauer*
You'll laugh and cry as Florence Littauer shares with you heart-warming accounts of the personal lives of some of our greatest leaders. Learn of their triumphs and tragedies, and become aware of the different personality patterns that exist and how our leaders have been influenced by them.
Discover your own strengths and weaknesses by completing the Personality Chart included in this book. *Personalities in Power* lets you understand yourself and others and helps you live up to your full potential.
ISBN 0-910311-56-0 $8.95

The Last Days Collection *by Last Days Ministries*
Heart-stirring, faith-challenging messages from Keith Green, David Wilkerson, Melody Green, Leonard Ravenhill, Winkie Pratney, Charles Finney and William Booth are designed to awaken complacent Christians to action.
ISBN 0-961-30020-5 $8.95

The Lucifer Connection *by Joseph Carr*
Shirley MacLaine and other celebrities are persuading millions that the New Age Movement can fill the spiritual emptiness in their lonely lives. Joseph Carr explains why the New Age Movement is the most significant and potentially destructive challenge to the church today. But is it new? How should Christians protect themselves and their children from this insidious threat? This book is a prophetic, information-packed examination by one of the most informed authors in America.
ISBN 0-910311-42-0 $7.95

Exposing the Aids Scandal: What You Don't Know Can Kill You *by Dr. Paul Cameron*
Where do you turn when those who control the flow of information in this country withhold the truth? Why is the national media hiding facts from the public? Can Aids be spread in ways we're not being told? Finally ... a book that gives you a total account of the Aids epidemic, and what steps can be taken to protect yourself. What you don't know can kill you!
ISBN 0-910311-52-8 $7.95

A Reasonable Reason to Wait *by Jacob Aranza*
God speaks specifically about premarital sex. Aranza provides a definite, frank discussion on premarital sex. He also provides a biblical healing message for those who have already been sexually involved before marriage. This book delivers an important message for young people, as well as their parents.
ISBN 0-910311-21-8 $5.95

Jubilee on Wall Street *by David Knox Barker*
On October 19, 1987, the New York Stock Exchange suffered its greatest loss in history — twice that of the 1929 crash. Will this precipitate a new Great Depression? This riveting book is a look at what the author believes is the inevitable collapse of the world's economy. Using the biblical principle of the Year of Jubilee, a refreshing dose of optimism and an easy-to-read style, the author shows readers how to avoid economic devastation.
ISBN 0-933-451-03-2 $7.95

America Betrayed *by Marlin Maddoux*
This hard-hitting book exposes the forces in our country which seek to destroy the family, the schools and our values. This book details exactly how the news media manipulates your mind. Marlin Maddoux is the host of the popular, national radio talk show "Point of View."
ISBN 0-910311-18-8 $6.95

The Great Falling Away Today *by Milton Green*
One of today's most talked-about teachers probes the spiritual condition of God's people. Thought-provoking reading for those concerned about sin and its effect on our fulfilling the Great Commission.
ISBN 0-910311-40-4 $6.95

Order These Books From Huntington House!